Death

And

Hell

The Two Places Every Human
Needs To Know About Before
Judgment Day,
Especially Christians

Minister Roderick Redd

Pastor of Christ Our Life Ministries

Wasteland Press
Louisville, KY USA
www.wastelandpress.net

Death And Hell
by Minister Roderick A. Redd

Second Printing – January 2008
ISBN: 978-1-60047-171-1

Printed in the U.S.A.

There is no greater torment or burning agony than to be separated from the presence of God. Not being in his presence is Hell and to be alienated from His light is eternal darkness. While the breath of life is in our nostrils, we must seek Jesus Christ. For he is the only doorway by which men are able to obtain entrance to God. Know that He is life and through Him we have eternal life.

Sister Stacie Coote
June 2004

Contents

All Scripture quotations are from the
King James Version Bible

About The Author

Minister Redd is a non-denominational ordained minister who was reared his entire life in the Lord by his mother. Upon completion of High School in 1983, he joined the US Army and strayed from his mother's upbringing and Biblical teachings. However, in 1993, while facing a dilemma in his marriage, Minister Redd rededicated his life to the Lord and confessed to the LORD that if He would restore his marriage, he would serve him faithfully for the remainder of his days on the earth. Within 6 months the LORD restored his marriage whole.

Since accepting his calling into the ministry, Minister Redd has preached in churches all around the world, taught Bible Study classes at his home, and assisted the V Corps Chaplain office in Heidelberg, Germany with its Gospel services while deployed in support of Operation Iraqi Freedom.

After serving for 22 years in the military, Minister Redd retired and moved to Augusta, Georgia, a place revealed to him in 1994 as the place he was to begin his ministry. A ministry God birthed in his spirit after he completed reading a book written by Watchman Nee entitled, "Christ Our Life".

On 16 December 2004, Minister Redd founded Christ Our Life Ministries and on 5 February 2006, the ministry held its first service. His vision for the ministry is to teach believers and unbelievers the truth about *Christ, the Spiritual Personality of Jesus who enables the believer to overcome the god of this world*.

Acknowledgments

First, Praises to God. For it was God who called me out of darkness and into His marvelous light in 1993 to a life I have truly fallen in love with, _the Christ Life_. Through this life, I have been given the strength, desire, and motivation to write this book and I count it an awesome privilege to be used of God to write a book of this magnitude.

A sincere heart of love and thanks to my wife, Dilay. Your constant question of _"when am I going to finish this book?"_ motivated me to utilize the time I normally waste watching television to bring this book to completion. I love you my tweety bird.

My two children, Reginald _(Daddy's Boogus-Boogus Man)_ and Esrene _(Daddy Baby)_. Without a doubt, you two are the instruments God used to transform me from an immature adult to a man of vision. Everything I do, I do as an example for you. Daddy loves his babies.

Much love to my mommy, Beatrice Martin. Everything I purpose to do is preceded with a question, _"What would my mother say if I did this?"_ This question has kept me out of so much trouble because I want you to see the fruit of your labour in my life. To my cousin, Rachel Martin. A true lover of God's Word. Your words of encouragement mean so much to me.

The best brothers and sisters in the world. Jeannie, Jackie, Bill, Chucky, Tommy, Ann, Darryl, David, and Michael. It is an honour having brothers and sisters who love each other with a fervent love and given me the best nephews and nieces in the world. True love in the highest degree.

To my-in-laws-the Goerguen family: Rasih, Ayla, and Dilhan. You have accepted me into your family and showered me with nothing but love since I married Dilay. I love you.

The best friend a man can have, Eddie Hall. I wish I could show you how much my heart appreciates the support you have given to me and the vision of Christ Our Life Ministries.

My Assistant pastor and his wife, Minister Kenya and Sister Dinah King. Minister King, God could not have given me a better right hand man. I wouldn't trade you for anyone. Sister King, you are and always will be the person in my eyes who I can talk to anything about, and never hear repeated. I appreciate your truthful and realness more than you will ever know. Your spirit is so hungry for God that it makes me seek God ever the more that you may receive the sound doctrine to satisfy that hunger.

My Ministry supporters; Stan and Selina Dychess, Warrant Officers Michael and Tracey Brooks, Sister Wendy Banks, Pastor Reginald Walker, Minister Jeffrey Scott, Evangelist Venessa Strong, Minister Damon Williams, Minister John Bethea, Minister Jose Sanchez, Minister Robert Blackstone, Minister Anthony Grant, Minister Roger and Prophetess Jamessica Joyner, Minister Gillis Taylor, Sister Marsha Carnegie, Sister Jackie Key, Sister Pamela Y. Smith, Brother Timothy Gilbert, Bother Everette and Sister Kim Smith, Deacon Randy Wilburn, and definitely, Mike Truax, my web master and God given friend who inspired me to step out in faith. Without your support, there would be no Christ Our Life Ministries in Augusta, Georgia.

My co-workers at PCS Nitrogen in Augusta, Georgia. My bosses, Warren Stroman and Virgil Fowler—I could not have asked God for better bosses. Mary Shore-Nobody has made me feel more welcomed at PCS than you, nobody. Erica Hanley—my buddy, and the most straight forward honest person I ever met; please don't change, the worlds needs more people like you. The SHE Department -Randall, Joey, Mark, Jamie, Lamar, and you too Rick Humphrey-my buddy, Joan Barsh. My security officers, Mason Morrow—my editor and right hand man, Cecil *"Flash"* Hunter, Edward *"Gunsmoke"* Adams, and Tito *"Cell Phone"* Rodriguez. My traffic family—Mary Mclean,

Connie Hankerson, Tonya *"too kind"* Kervin, Charles Brightharp, Cindy Hallford, Sharon Coachman, and Lisa Kersey.

Last but not least, my Pastor, Lewis Gurley. Pastor of ***Abundant Life in the Word Church***, located in Lawton, Oklahoma, and his lovely wife, Niecy. Your exceptional hunger for God placed such a conviction on me when I did not attempt to embrace the standard you set for yourself. You taught me how to study the Word and I thank you for that. Pleasing God is my first priority in Life. The second is to live a life based on the principles you lived by and taught me so that you will see that your labour in me was not in vain. I love you Pastor.

Preface

This book is addressed to every human walking the face of the earth, especially those professing to be Christians. Why? Because there are millions of humans, but most importantly, born-again believers living on the earth who do not have the slightest idea of how to differentiate between two places that every human has heard of yet lack a great deal of knowledge about and the name of these two places are **Death** and **Hell**. Now, due to the lack of knowledge that men possess regarding **Death** and **Hell**, Satan, the embodiment of evil and *"the god of this world (2Cor 4:4)"* works hard to keep our mind in darkness. This work has kept men from obtaining the knowledge we need to see these two places from a spiritual perspective and their future location in eternity.

Now, I personally believe that today's church leaders, *including myself at times* have not diligently sought God arduously enough to receive the spiritual knowledge needed to teach humans about **Death** and **Hell** so that it will prompt mankind into thinking twice about God's great salvation plan for humanity and the consequences associated with **Death** and **Hell**,. Therefore, I pray that through this book all of us will be quickened in our inner man to set aside a portion of **Time** to get in the presence of God so that we may receive instructions in righteousness *(2Tim 3:16)*. Instructions that'll illuminate the minds of men whether it be us who attend church services consistently on a weekly basis or those who have no desire to attend church services at all but believe there is a God. The **Time** has come for *the Body of Christ* to stop preaching those same old weekly messages *that almost every religious channel on Television is preaching and teaching*. Messages that minister more to our outer-most *(earthen vessel)* man and it's **Fleshly** lust than to our inner-most *(Spirit)* man because it is the Spirit man within us who seeks after the Kingdom of God and all His righteousness as mentioned in *Matt 6:33*.

1

So, according to _Romans 13:11 & Ephesians 5:16,_ our **Time** is **now**. Now for us to minister unto the Body of Christ and unbelievers exactly what Our Lord and Saviour Jesus Christ said in _Revelation 1:18_ when he told the Apostle John, _"I am he that liveth, and was dead; and, behold, I am alive for evermore, Amen; and have **the keys of Hell and of Death**."_ Note, the Lord makes a separate distinction regarding these two places and says, **_"keys"_**, not key. Why are there two keys and what do these keys have to do with me as a born-again believer? Why does the Lord speak this word unto the Seven Churches when I have been told that if I believe in the name of the Lord Jesus and call upon His name that I will be saved and live in Heaven? God's Word clearly answers these questions. So, by the anointing of the Holy Spirit on my life and through the words of this book, my intention is to impart unto you what the Spirit has revealed unto me that I believe should be ministered to every human being living on this earth concerning **Death and Hell**, especially Christians.

My objective is to fill this book with an abundance of Bible verses. I will not write out every verse because I want you to read the Bible for yourself. I want you to see how important it is for you to know what The Holy Bible says with your own eyes because The Holy Bible _is really_ the only book a human needs that will answer every question they desire an answer to, while at the same **Time** being drawing them nearer to God and drawing God nearer to them. I also believe that men and women of God who write spiritual books receive this knowledge from God in part to the **Time** they've spent studying His Holy Word. However, _1Cor 13:9 &12_ does tell us to trust no man, including myself. Don't trust me. Trust God. My prayer is that through this book God will quicken you in your spirit-man and impart unto you revelation knowledge about **Death and Hell** that you never heard before but hungered and thirsted to know _(Matt 5:6)_. I hope this book blesses you abundantly.

Introduction

Since answering the call of God on my life in 1993 and receiving licensure as a minister in 1997 (*Ordained in 2004*), God has blessed me in ways I never thought imaginable. During those times of blessings, I've had the privilege of fellowshipping with many believers all around the world *(in the military for 22 years)* who love God with an everlasting love but have also voiced their disappointment in regards to the lack of spirituality ministered in many of today's church services. This disappointment burdens the Spirit within me for I know deep down inside that many of today's church leaders *(Ephesians 4:11-13 and Romans 12:4-7)* have a desire to minister in this manner just as myself but the enemy of our souls and God oppresses so many of us to where worldliness has made its way into our church services and the effects of its entrance is causing many believers to receive an erroneous word not from God that brings no victory to the life of a believer. I am a teacher of God's Word and I know the teachings of *Romans 12:3* and *1Corinthians 9:27*. Therefore, I will be ever mindful of these two verses of scripture as I allow the Spirit of God to minister to you about ***Death and Hell***.

While on assignment in Heidelberg, Germany, a beloved brother of mine, Minister Jose Sanchez, called me from Fort Drum, New York inquiring about ***Hell***. As I began to answer his question, the Holy Spirit spoke a word through me concerning Death and Hell that I had never heard before but was as clear to me as water. The spiritual impartation of knowledge from God through me was so profound that I began to tremble. Since receiving the impartation of this word, I have a new found reverence for the Word of God *(Heb 10:26)* that I dare not disobey and after reading this book, I pray that you will be likeminded.

Now, before you begin reading the first chapter of this book, I need to lay a foundation that you must give the most earnest heed and not allow anything to distract your mind from it. First, the number one thing I need for you to remember about God is mentioned in *Num 23:19*. Why? Because according to *Heb 6:18*, it is impossible for God to lie. Secondly, the church that most of us attend today is filled with converted Gentiles *(I have encountered converted Jews)*. Gentiles who once walked a certain way as told to us in *Eph 4:17-18* but have now answered the call of God on their life and submitted themselves unto the voice of His Son, Jesus Christ *(Heb 1:1-2)*. Notice, I did not say that they are commanded to hearken unto the voice of the fathers *(Abraham-John8:58/Acts7:2)* or the prophets, including Moses, as mentioned in *Matt 17:1-5*, or the Law as mentioned in *Gal 3:19-29* that God spoke to Moses so that he may deliver it to the twelve tribes of Israel. *(God never covenanted with a gentile nation or gave them His laws (Psalms 147:19-20)*. Therefore, having read this, I pray that from hence forth, you will not be confused as to whose words born again believers should be in obedience to *(Matt 17:1-5)*.

Christ Jesus is the **only man** *(The Lamb of God)* that God has sent with the words *(John 6:68)* to save men from the penalty of eternal damnation and separation from God. He is the **only man** who has the power to resurrect from the **Dead**, to give **Life**, to cast into **Hell**, and the **only man** who died and rose and is going to return to this planet as Lord of lords and King of kings to judge this world in righteousness not the teachings of the law. Now, who have you heard or know of in the Bible other than Jesus that has a testimony like this? What makes Jesus different than any other man?

According to *1Cor 15:45* Jesus Christ, our Lord and Savior was born a quickening Spirit but *Gen 2:7* tells us that the first man Adam, our father, was *born a living soul* but sinned and is in need of rebirth according to the Word of God by Water and of the Spirit as told to Nicodemus by Jesus in *John 3:5-7*. Why? In the beginning, the first man Adam, our father, disobeyed the commandment of the Lord God. His disobedience caused every human born of flesh and blood to enter this world with his image; the image of a sinner. An image alienated from the Life of God as told in *Eph 4:17-18*, living in a cursed earthen vessel that will one day return to the dust of the earth from whence it came (*Gen 2:7, 3:19*).

What you've read are *facts,* not theories. Therefore, having read and prayerfully understood what was previously written, the most important thing I want unbelievers as well as born-again believers to know is this, ***Until Judgment Day arrives, any human who dies without accepting Jesus Christ as Lord and Saviour of his/her life, will be held in Death. Whereas, Hell will be the holding cell for any born-again believer who Sins willfully after coming into the knowledge of the truth and dies without confessing his/her sins and obtaining forgiveness of those Sins (Heb 10:26 and Luke 13:24-28)***.

And the LORD answered me, and said, Write the vision, and make it plain upon tables, that he may run that readeth it. For the vision is yet for an appointed time, but at the end it shall speak, and not lie: though it tarry, wait for it; because it will surely come, it will not tarry.

Habakkuk 2:2-3

Man's Dilemma

*Wherefore, as by one man sin entered into the world
and death by sin; and so death passed upon
all men, for that all have sinned*
Romans 5:12

Dilemma, what dilemma? Yes, this is the natural response of most human beings *(souls)* today as the Word of God forewarns men and women about the world and the life of the earthy body we are born with. Nevertheless, reality has painted us a clear picture that most of the human populace even after having heard the Word of God and His great salvation plan for mankind, continue to live as though there is nothing appealing about the Word of God that'll make them want to exchange their present day lifestyle for a spiritual lifestyle proclaimed in *Romans 14:17* as a life filled with *"righteousness, joy, and peace in the Holy Ghost"*. Now, I know for a ***fact*** that most of these humans will tell you that they have accepted Jesus Christ as Lord and Savior of their life, to include many that are church leaders who profess that God called them into the Gospel ministry. Yet, the lifestyle they exhibit before the world contradicts the very words their mouths (*Romans 10:9-10*) speak. Words that have given our nation's newspaper, radio, and television stations an untrue report (*Isaiah 53:1*) of what Christianity truly is while at the same ***Time*** bringing our Lord and Savior Jesus Christ and His Church to an open shame.

Now, Merriam-Webster's dictionary defines the word ***fact*** as, *"a thing done or an actual occurrence"*. The certainty that individuals who profess Jesus Christ as Lord and Savior of their life need to read and ask God to give them an understanding of the lesson taught in *Proverbs 6:2* and confess their ***Sins*** *(1John 1:9)* before they experience ***Death*** and have to face ***God's judgment*** as mentioned in *Hebrews 9:27*. Our nation's newspaper, radio, and television stations have exposed Bishops, Pastors, Prophets, and other born-again believers who confess Jesus Christ to be the Lord and Savior of their life but in ***fact***

6

have not submitted themselves **completely** to any of _His sayings and teachings_. Now, what in the world is it in people that bewitches _(Gal 3:1)_ a man or woman to live a lifestyle that propels him or her to rebel against the Word of God that they know to be **fact**? I'll tell you what it is, it is **Sin**, the **nature and personality** of Satan himself and all of us are born into this world slaves to this **nature** _(Romans 5:12)_. Furthermore, this **nature** is defined in _Romans 7:21-24_, as a law. A law that is no different than the law of gravity. You cannot see gravity but gravity is at work twenty four hours a day holding things on the earth. **Sin**, man's inherent **nature** is no different. It is a law that holds men in disobedience to the commandments of God; a law mingled together with our created earth suit; working twenty four hours a day _(1John 1:8-9)_ to ensure that we live rebelliously to one another and ignorant of God's salvation plan for us. Now, my intentions for this book is to give enlightenment to your mind on several things that Satan via **Sin** uses to oppress mankind _(2Cor 4:3-5)_ in order to keep men alienated from the life of God _(Christ)_ and the things I shall expound on are **Time, Care, Flesh and Sin, Death, and Hell.**

One might ask, "How did we get put into this **Dilemma**?" We are in this **Dilemma** because of the disobedience of one man, the first man Adam _(Romans 5:12 - 1Cor 15:45)_. Satan, the enemy of God and mankind, through cunning ways deceived the first man Adam's wife, Eve into eating of the forbidden tree which the Lord God had given **commandment** not to eat of, then Eve gave it to her husband, the first man Adam, _who was not deceived (I Tim 2:14)_ and they ate _(Gen 3:6)_. Once the first man Adam committed this trespass, his actions combined **Sin**, the nature of Satan with **Flesh** _(Genesis 6:1-5)_. Before the first man Adam and Eve ate of the forbidden tree, their bodies were of the dust but they did not notice it. After they ate of the forbidden tree, the dust became conscious of itself and the law of **Sin** that now governs it gives mankind the knowledge of "_good and evil_" _(Gen 3:22)_. Let's look at _Genesis 3:22_ and see what the Lord God says about men. He says,

7

"And the Lord God said, Behold, the man is become as one of us, to know good and evil: and now, lest he put forth his hand, and take also of the tree of life, and eat, and live for ever."

The Lord God says that when men became **Flesh**, they received the knowledge of *"good and evil."* They did not become as the Lord God in personality, but they now possessed the knowledge of the Lord God and that knowledge was the knowledge of *"good and evil" (Rom 7:14-25)*. In this book, I will refer to the **Flesh** sometimes as *Earth Suit*. The dictionary definition of the word **Flesh** is, "*the body as distinct from the soul*", *something separate yet living*. How can this be, the **Flesh**, cannot exist without the soul? The first man Adam, who was made a living soul *(1Cor 15:45)*, **willfully** disobeyed the LORD God and ate of the forbidden tree. Wherefore, in *Gen. 3:7-10*, you can read that immediately upon the first man Adam's partaking of the forbidden tree, how the Glory of God departed from him and his wife. This departure changed his Lord God formed dust suit from a glorified vessel into a **Fleshly** self-conscious vessel. In addition, his disobedience transformed his spiritual **personality/mind** that only knew life and walked by faith *(what it could not see)* *(Rom 12:1-2)*, into a carnal **personality/mind** that walked by sight and not by faith *(what it could see)*.

Now, Webster's dictionary defines Carnal as *"having a relationship to the body"*; **Fleshly**. Men now had a relationship with the **Flesh** and not with the LORD God, and the reason why we are in a **Dilemma** today. Look at *Genesis 3:7-8*, it says,

*"And the eyes of them both were opened, **and they knew that they were naked**; and they sewed fig leaves together, and made themselves aprons. And they heard the voice of the LORD God walking in the garden in the cool of the day: and Adam and his wife hid themselves from the presence of the LORD God amongst the trees of the garden."*

Prior to their transgression, neither the first man Adam nor Eve possessed the knowledge of earthly nakedness even though they were naked. They were created with a conscience completely void of carnality. It wasn't until they ate of the forbidden tree that they became **conscience of themselves** and carnal nakedness. After receiving this new impartation of knowledge, the first man Adam and Eve sewed fig leaves together to cover their nakedness. Today, **Sin** has people uncovering their *Earth Suits*. Nakedness and sexuality is the most dominate thought in the world today, and if you were to look at the attire of some of the believers, you would not think they knew anything about modest apparel *(1Tim 2:9)*.

    Dilemma number one, God did not crown the fig tree or its leaves with glory and honor. God crowned Adam and Eve, and only men with glory and honor. The new impartation of knowledge they gained from the forbidden tree now guided their thoughts and actions. Those thoughts made them "*lean to their own understanding*" *(Prov. 3:5-7)* and cover themselves with fig leaves in hopes that they could hide their shame and maintain a relationship with the LORD God. Instead, they soon realized that this new personality actually caused them to fear the presence of the LORD God. These souls, which previously had been governed and joined unto each other and the LORD by faith *(Romans 10:17)* was now deadened (*Ephesians 2:1*) to the thoughts and ways of the LORD *(Isaiah 55:7-8)*.

    In *Romans 7:14 and Matt 6:24* we can see that their **Flesh**, which the bible calls, "*the body of Sin*" *(Rom 6:6)* now ruled their minds and became their master *(Rom 7:14)*. Within a moment of a twinkling of the eye, the first man Adam and Eve found themselves in a **_Dilemma_** and afraid of the one who had given them life and loved them without measure.

    Neither Adam nor Eve was to have a relationship with their earth suit. They were created by God to live a spiritual life; the life God created for them in *Genesis 1:27-28* that reads,

"So God created man in his own image, in the image of God created he him; male and female created he them. And God blessed them, and God said unto them, Be fruitful, and multiply,

and replenish the earth, and subdue it: and have dominion over the fish of the sea, and over the fowl of the air, and over every living thing that moveth upon the earth."

God, who is Spirit, does not have relationships with earth suits. In *fact*, it is the Lord God who has relationships with earth suits. No where in Genesis chapter one will you find God speaking to a dust-formed earth suit. ***God created man (Male/Female) in His image for man to contain and fellowship with Him in Spirit and in Truth.*** Notice, I said to be a ***contain***er. A container is *"Something one stores things in"*. Have you ever read *Romans 10:17*? It says, *"Faith cometh by hearing, and hearing by the word of God"*. Whenever something comes, the purpose of it coming is to be received and contained. So, after God created these male/female containers, ***God said unto them***, *Be fruitful, and multiply, and replenish the earth, and* **subdue it: and have dominion over** *the fish of the sea, and over the fowl of the air, and over* **every living thing that moveth upon the earth**. This command is not a command intended for our earth suit. We are not in Genesis chapter two yet. This is God depositing His will into the eternal man *(2Cor 4:18)*; the Word *(John 1:1)* created un-seeable male/female containers.

Now, in *Genesis 2:7*, we see that it was the *LORD God who formed the eternal man's earth suit* from the *"dust of the earth"*. After forming the earth suit, the eternal man whom God had created was deposited into the earth suit through the nostrils by the LORD God. Once this created eternal man inhabited the earth suit, the earth suit became a living soul. A soul possessing the ability to have physical contact with the planet through the ***Flesh*** and spiritual contact   with the spiritual world through belief in the Words of the LORD God and the Tree of Life. This eternal man was given the name of Adam by the LORD God. The first man Adam's partaking of the fruit produced by the Tree of Life would have provided Adam with the knowledge he would need for Him, the LORD God, and Eve to enjoy a life full of love and happiness together just as a married couple is supposed to do. Now, you do know what the purpose of marriage is, right? Well, the purpose of marriage is for when a male and female (*not two-male or two-female Gen 1:27*) personalities contained in separate earth suits formed of dust by the LORD God, fall in love and decide they want to live together, *forever*, until **Death** do them part in a covenant relationship *(a spiritually minded person knows that the breaking of a covenant always results in spiritual death)*. A life that excludes everyone except themselves and the covenant between them. Don't let **Sin** bewitch you until you become ignorant of the vows individuals confess to each other at marriages when they say, "**Until Death do us part**." (*Prov 6:2*). There are too many earth suits alive today living in violation of this vow.

Have you ever met anyone who finds pleasure when **Death** touches someone in their life that they love? I don't and if I said I did, I would be lying. However, it is a proven *fact* in today's society that divorce is rampant. Even more alarming is the *fact* that some of those divorces are by individuals who profess to have a relationship with Christ. Now, divorce is the word men use for terminating a marriage, but divorce is just a nicer way of killing a covenant *(Matt 19:3-9)*. The Lord God hates divorce because it symbolizes **Death** to Him. Why? **Death** separates the living from the living. In other words, when two individuals are covenanted together and one commits a trespass, the trespass committed kills the covenant founded on love; founded on words of truth *(Prov 6:2)* and because one of the marriage partners transgressed, it opened a doorway for **Death** to enter the relationship and destroy it *(John 10:10)* or the one trespassed against forgives the trespasser of that trespass *(Matt 6:15)*. So, when the first man Adam trespassed against the commandment of the LORD God, he died and according to *Romans 5:12*, "*by one man Sin entered into the world, and Death by Sin; and so Death passed upon all men, for that all have Sinned*". The first man Adam's act of disobedience made all men trespassers and sinners in the eyesight of God, wherefore we all die.

God's perfect will in creation was not for us to know **Death**. God's will was for mankind to live and enjoy fellowship with Him. His will was not for mankind to be a slave of **Sin** and

11

experience **Death**. God's will was for mankind to rule the earth with Christ as their life but in order for God's will to be done, the first man Adam had to *obey the sayings and teachings* of the LORD God. If the first man Adam did not eat of the forbidden tree, God knew the fruit they would eat from the tree of life would keep the relationship between He and mankind alive forever. The marriage relationship between the first man Adam, the LORD God, and Eve with Christ as their life was never supposed to end. However, *Romans 5:12-17* tells us that Satan's deceptive plan and Adam's willful decision *(1Tim 2:14)* to eat of the Tree of the knowledge of Good and Evil brought **Death** into the relationship putting it asunder and in turn opened a doorway for **Death** to enter this world and reign in all earth suits whether it be man or beast *(Gen 6:7)*. For all men are partakers of the first Adam's **Flesh** and blood *(Hebrews 2:14)*. Well, why beast? Read *Genesis 3:14*, the serpent was a beast.

Every human born of the earth with the exception of Christ Jesus, was conceived through a relationship involving a male/female earth suit. No human has arrived on this planet without the **Flesh** and blood of the first man Adam and it does not matter what color or race you are. This however, does not apply to Christ Jesus. Christ Jesus is the last Adam *(1Cor 15:45-47)*. The first man Adam is of the earth, earthy: the last Adam, Christ Jesus, is the Lord from heaven. Let's look at *1Corinthians 15:45-47*. It reads,

*"And so it is written, the **first man Adam** was made a living soul; the **last Adam** was made a quickening spirit. Howbeit that was not first which is spiritual, but that which is natural; and afterward that which is spiritual. The first man is of the earth, earthy: the second man is the Lord from heaven."*

Here we have the first man Adam and the last Adam. Jesus, who is the Christ. The last Adam, Christ, ended the first man Adam's reign in the earth suit (Phil 1:21). Our belief in Him opens a doorway *(Acts 14:27)* for us to receive Christ as our life; the everlasting life that God intended for mankind to have from the beginning. Christ's **_Death on the cross_** destroyed *(Rom 6:6)* the first man Adam image life *(carnal)* passed to us from the first man Adam *(Gen 5:3)*. Note, I am not going to hold Eve responsible for the **Dilemma** humans are in because Eve was in the loins of the first man Adam *(His Rib)* when the LORD God commanded Adam not to eat of the forbidden tree. So, whether Eve ate of the forbidden tree deceitfully or willfully, she was the first man Adam. Let's read *Genesis 2:21-23*, they read,

"And the LORD God caused a deep sleep to fall upon Adam and he slept: and he took one of his ribs, and closed up the flesh instead thereof; And the rib, which the LORD God had taken from man, made he a woman, and brought her unto the man. And Adam said this is now bone of my bones, and flesh of my flesh: she shall be called Woman, because she was taken out of Man."

Now if Eve had been taken from the dust of the earth apart from Adam like everything else, I would have mentioned her but she wasn't. She was *taken from* the earth suit of the first man Adam and confessed by the first man Adam to be *bone of my bones, and flesh of my flesh*. The LORD God never went back to the earth to form her. He formed her solely from Adam's rib; her skin, everything about her earth suit from one rib. Why did the first man Adam say *this is now bone of my bones, and flesh of my flesh*? Not every earth suit creature has bones, especially serpents. That's why *Hebrews 4:12* says,

"For the word of God is quick, and powerful, and sharper than any two-edged sword, piercing even to the dividing asunder of soul and spirit, and of the joints and marrow, and is a discerner of the thoughts and intents of the heart."

Marrow is *a soft vascular tissue that fills the cavities of most bones*. The Word of God has to go that deep in some of us *(Job 12:22, Psalms 42:7)* in order to save us from ourselves. The Lord God goes deep within us and blesses us with things already in us; he places the future of everything within itself and the last thing the Lord God blesses the first man Adam with after He had given him everything He had created *(Gen 2:18-20)* was Eve.

Why did the LORD God do this? The LORD God made this female earth suit for the first man Adam so that he would have an earthly companion to rule the earth with. But, *Genesis 1:27* tells us the main reason for Eve's earth suit creation. It is because **God had created** an eternal female personality that had not yet received an earth suit container to dominate the earth with. Furthermore, *Genesis 5:1-2* teaches us something also. When **God created** these male and female spirit personalities, He, being God, the Spirit, called their name Adam in the day they were **created**. Notice, ***this married couple had the same last name***. I hope this sheds some light for men and women who marry but choose to retain the name they possessed prior to being joined in Holy matrimony *(Josh 24:15)*. People who marry after this manner prove that independence exist in their marriage above togetherness and submission *(Eph 5:22/Col 3:18)*. I know some of you don't like that but the truth is the truth. Humble yourself and change your name, don't get to angry at me, you might **Sin** *(Eph 4:26)*.

The first man Adam's partaking of the Tree of the knowledge of Good and Evil **annulled the covenant** between himself, God the Father, the Word *(John 1:14)*, and the Holy Spirit *(1John 5:7)*. It even caused division in *Genesis 3:7* regarding the first man Adam and Eve's marriage relationship *(married couples are not ashamed to see each other naked)*. Furthermore, we are told in *Genesis 3:22-24* that the first man Adam and Eve's transgression caused the LORD God to drive them out of the Garden of Eden (*lest he should partake of the Tree of Life and live forever Genesis 3:22*) and into the *wilderness*. Wilderness is defined as "*a region uncultivated and uninhabited by human beings*." There weren't any other humans on earth at that time to do any cultivating. You Scientologist better hear what the Word of God is saying *(John 8:32)* since you think you know science and creation so well.

The Lord God's driving of the first man Adam and Eve from the Garden should not come as a surprise to anybody. Look at what happens when people get divorced in our world today. One of the partners is driven out of the house. In *Genesis 2:8* it says that *"The Lord God planted a garden eastward in Eden; and there he put the man whom he had formed.* So, the driving out of the first man Adam and Eve from the Garden had to be done. Why? Because the first man Adam was not watching over his house and the Serpent deceived his wife who in turn gave him of the same fruit, who was with her at the **Time** *(Gen 3:6, and gave also unto her husband with her)* and he willfully took it and ate it. If the first man Adam *had known in what watch the thief would come, he would not have suffered his house to be broken (Matt 24:43).* He would have been paying attention to Eve's behaviors *(Phil 4:6).* His willful transgression mingled Satan's sinful nature (*we will discuss this in Chapter 4*) with their earth suit, giving **Sin** a place for habitation *(Romans 7:17).* This turned the first man Adam and Eve's bodies into *bodies of Sin (Rom 6:6)* filled with uncleanness and iniquities *(Rom 6:19).* They also became the servants of these bodies and the **Sin** in them made them rebel against everything the LORD God desired of them. So, the LORD God drove them out of the garden lest they continue to feed themselves along with the *body of Sin* from the tree of life and the *body of Sin* lives forever.

Now, since the day the LORD God drove the first man Adam and Eve from the Garden of Eden, the godhead has been trying to get men to reject the evil thoughts Satan oppresses them with concerning Christ Jesus, God's only begotten Son but men do not **Believe** what God or His Word says about Christ Jesus. Do you know what God's Word says about Christ Jesus, His only begotten Son? It says,

"*For God so loved the world, that he gave his only begotten Son, that whosoever believeth in him should not perish, but have everlasting life (John 3:16).*"

Believe! Yes, believe. This is the hurdle men are having the hardest **Time** trying to conquer. Why? Because the life we inherited from the first man Adam made us servants of the earth suit we were born in. Earth suits known that the Bible calls, *the body of Sin (Rom 6:6).* In addition, it must servants to the god of this world, Satan. Satan in turn, keeps men in darkness blinding their minds to prevent mankind from believing God's word, lest the light of the glorious gospel of Jesus Christ, who is the image of God, should shine unto them *(2Cor. 4:4)*. Then, he tempts men with the things of this world; things that make it hard for men to **believe** the Word of God *(Jesus, John 1:14)* because Satan knows that our belief in the Word of God is the one way men are able to overcome him and his temptations. We have to start believing now, because **Time** is running out on us and this world is about to be judged.

The Bible is filled with testimonies of humans who have doubted the words spoken by the fathers, prophets, and the LORD God *(Heb 1:1-2)*. Our generation today is no different despite the **fact** that God's Word is being preached extensively. Let me give you a testimony about a day in my life when I doubted. I doubt sometimes too *(1Cor 9:27)*.

One day while on flag detail putting up the unit flag in front of our headquarters building, I mistakenly raised the flag upside down. Upon walking away from the flag pole, a Deacon and dear sister in the LORD, also in my unit looking from their office window, told me that I had raised the flag upside down. I said, "Yeah, you wish, you'll never fool me, I've raised that flag correctly for the last 9 days, you'll never make me think I did it wrong this time and I am not looking up to see if I did it wrong because I know I put the flag up right, you can't fool me." I did not look up either. Then, another sister in the LORD walking out the building said, you should check just to make sure, I said "I know I put that flag up right and I'm not looking up either". Upon entering my office to begin work, the Deacon came to me and said, "Master Sergeant Redd, I was not lying, you did raise the flag upside down." As I began to visualize my actions, I saw that I did hang the flag in the correct position, but connected the bottom clamp used for holding the bottom of the flag to the top of the flag thereby making the Deacon's story true. I thanked the Deacon, repented, and corrected the flag.

Do you as a Christian sometimes doubt the words of those you know to be of the family of God? If your answer is yes, *then* this unbelief problem must be overcome because our failure to **believe** the truth *(John 17:17)* from the Word of God or from those we know to be of the body of Christ means that you and I are not going to trust and obey it. In addition, failure to obey the truth of God's Word will hinder us from entering God's rest *(Heb 3:10-13)* and eliminating any chance of us escaping **Death** *(Ezek 18:4)* or being tormented in **Hell** *(Matt 10:28)*. However, like I said at the beginning of this chapter, the outward lifestyles on display by millions of humans' prove that men do not *believe in* the Word of God or the forewarnings of God and while they continue to live in unbelief, ***the Time for them to accept Christ Jesus as Lord and Saviour of their life is running out***.

Time

*To every thing there is a season, and a __Time__
to every purpose <u>Under</u> the heaven
Ecc 3:1*

While attending elementary, middle, and high school, I was taught that the earth is located in the Milky Way Galaxy. However, while studying the Word of God, I discovered that earth is located in **_Time_**. Now, the dictionary defines **_Time_** as, "*a period during which an action, process, or condition exists or continues*" and we know that there comes a **_Time_** in a person's life when *an action, process, or condition seizes to exist* and this *action, process, or condition* I shall address is the **_Time_** of a male/female's *(Gen 1:27)* life on the earth.

According to *Genesis 6:3*, Moses, the servant of the Lord *(Joshua 1:1-2)* who wrote the first five books of the Bible, records this Word from the Lord God concerning a man's life on the Earth, "__*My spirit shall not always strive with man*__, *for that he also is **Flesh**: yet **his days shall be an hundred and twenty years***" and in *Psalm 90:10*, Moses says in his prayer to the LORD, "*The days of our years are **threescore years and ten (70)**; and if by reason of strength they **be fourscore years (80)**, yet is their strength labour and sorrow; for <u>it is soon cut off, and we fly away</u>*". Has anyone ever told you this? Have those who you submit the keeping of your soul to informed you of this? Well, they should have. In addition, I also want you to know that **_Time and Earth are under_** the heaven and at the completion of this chapter, you will be thanking God that they are.

According to *Daniel 8:19/12:4&9*, it is written that **_Time is not eternal;_** and in *Mark13:31 / Luke21:33 / Rev21:1*, we discover that the **_Earth is not eternal_** either. Yet, humans are living as though they have all the **_Time_** in the world to do whatever they want unaware of the **_fact_** that **_Time_** is steadily running out on them for establishing a relationship with God.

Now, this is something Satan hopes they never will become aware of while at the same **_Time_** causing their souls to go through all kinds of trials laden with all sorts of problems. He has some believing that riches will solve many of their problems but riches cannot do that. Why? Because according to _1John 5:19,_ the world we live in lieth in wickedness, in Satan Satan's world. A world where Satan is able to tempts them with all kinds of temptations and they desire more things; things that men exalt above God's Word _(Phil 4:19)_. Things that cause many to believe they will experience days overflowing with money and everything goes as they desire. However, Satan has no intentions of ever allowing them to live and experience that life. Now, that is wickedness. Satan however, will allow some people to get money, but believe me, he'll ensure that they do not spend it as their heart desires _(Prov 19:21)._ Instead, he will ensure that their life is void of good health, a perfect marriage, or friends who never betray them. Furthermore, in the life of a believer, he's going to make sure that you and I never come to a point in life where we are content _(1Tim 6:6)_ with the things God has blessed us with.

Now, this **_wanting_** that believers and unbelievers desire is a wanting to live a **_Care_**-free life. Yes, a **_Care_**-free life would be heavenly wouldn't it (_We will talk about **Care** in the next chapter_)? However, in this world, Satan intends to see that you and I live a life filled with tribulations because Satan actually hates you. Why? Because God loves you and as long as you have the breath of life in your nostrils _(Gen 2:7),_ Satan knows that God will do everything to save you, even if it means sacrificing _His Only Begotten Son_. Why do you think Satan took upon himself the form of a serpent to beguile Eve in the Garden of Eden? Why did Satan do this? Satan hates God; God cast him out of heaven for rebelling against Him and Satan knew the way he could get some type of revenge against God was to steal _(John 10:10)_ the only creature created in the image of God for containing God on the earth _(Eph 2:22)._ Satan therefore devised a plan to steal mankind from God and use their earthen body to oppress mankind into worshipping him instead of worshipping God. So, he tempted Eve to eat of the forbidden tree which she and her husband did. Satan knew that if the first man Adam and Eve disobeyed the commandment of the LORD God, he would be able to oppress them to obey him through their earth suit the same way he controlled the serpent's earth suit. By doing this, Satan again could wage war against God. Satan's plan worked, the first humans **disobeyed the commandment**. Answer this question. *"Have you ever had something extremely dear to your heart stolen from you? Well, if you have and it deeply hurt you, then God feels that same way about men who have been stolen from Him yet do not return to him when he calls out to them (Rev 3:20)."*

So, in *Romans 5:19* we are told that after the first man Adam and Eve disobeyed the commandment of the LORD God, all men were made sinners and became allies with Satan. This act caused Satan, the first man Adam, and Eve to become one in body, one in thought, one in expression, and according to *Ecclesiastes 4:12*, a threefold cord; a cord that is not easily broken which is why in *Genesis, Chapter 3*, the LORD God cursed this threefold cord but He cursed them individually. Did you read that, individually? The LORD God is the only one who can break a threefold cord. Yet, if you were to look at the attitudes of most men and women today, including those who profess to be born-again, you would think that not even the LORD is able to break this cord. Furthermore, this threefold cord is a major reason why our world lieth in wickedness and the strength of it is the *law of Sin (Rom 7:23)* and it causes men to look on outward appearances of everything *(1Sam 16:7)*.

This evil threefold cord has humanity bound in crimes, murders, terrorism, and most importantly, racism. Nevertheless, God has this threefold cord bound in **Time**, *"a period during which an action, process, or condition exists or continues.* God has also appointed a day that He will end **Time**. On that day, this threefold cord will not only be forever broken, it will be forever destroyed *(Mark 1:24, Luke 4:34)*.

Do you know a male or female who can stop the wicked conditions men are faced with today? Let me answer that for you, No!! The uniting of Satan, the first man Adam, and Eve made all men sinners and turned this world into a wicked place and according to *James 4:4*, the enemies of God. So, read *James 4:4* and ask yourself a question, "*Am I a friend of the world*?" This is a question that only you can answer and when the breath of life departs your earth suit *(Heb 9:27)*, answer it you shall.

We as humans know there are rich and boastful people living on this earth who are allowing Satan to control every area of their lives, living as though they will never experience a troublesome day *(Gangs, Mafia)*. All you have to do is look at the way they live and our Hollywood Movie Stars too. In addition, look at some of our world known television evangelists. They do not appear to have a *Care (worry)* in this world for the souls they are accountable for while at the same *Time* living a luxurious life financed by the wages earned by their church members *(Mal 3:5)*. However, no one is prone to tribulations. *Sin* and *Death* will make sure of that. How? Through the process of *Time*. *Sin*, which is a law (*I will explain this law in chapter 4*) waits for the right *Time* to strike when men least expect it and when it strikes, according to *James 1:15*, *Death* occurs. Now, even though many people reading this know that what I am saying to be *fact*, most of them continue to live sinful lives, including some believers but the Apostle Paul has a warning for these people. In *Phil 4:6*, he warns men to "*Be careful for nothing; but in every thing by prayer and supplication with thanksgiving let your requests be made known unto God*". This is a spiritual principle. How many people do you believe apply this principle in their life on a daily basis? Let me help you. How often do you *by prayer and supplication with thanksgiving let your requests be made known unto God*?

Let's look at Genesis, Chapter 4, and visit Cain, the *first born child of the first man Adam* and see if he rejected the *sayings and teachings of the Lord (Hosea 4:6)*. This first born son of the first man Adam did not hearken unto the LORD when the LORD spoke to him about *Sin* and the hatred he had towards his brother Abel. Verses 3-8, read,

"*And in **process of Time** it came to pass, that Cain brought of the fruit of the ground an offering unto the LORD. And Abel, he also brought of the firstlings of his flock and of the fat thereof. And the LORD had respect unto Abel and to his offering: (5) But unto Cain and to his offering he had not respect. And Cain was very wroth, and his countenance fell. (6) And the LORD said unto Cain, Why art thou wroth? and why is thy countenance fallen? (7) if thou doest well, shalt thou not be accepted? and if thou doest not well, sin lieth at the door. And unto thee shall be his desire, and thou shalt rule over him. (8) And Cain talked with Abel his brother: and it came to pass, when they were in the field, that Cain rose up against Abel his brother, and slew him.*"

In verse 5, Cain's decision to present unto the LORD an offering **he thought** *(Prov 3:5-7)* was pleasing to the LORD was not respected. *If somebody brought you something you did not approve of, would you respect it*? Let me answer that for you, **No!!** The lack of respect the LORD had towards Cain's offering angered Cain. Now, according to *Ephes. 4:26*, that says, "*Be ye angry, and sin not: let not the sun go down upon your wrath*" proves that Cain lacked this knowledge and the **Sin** in Cain's earth suit vexed Cain until it drove him to slay his brother. The LORD knew exactly what it was in Cain that made him angry but at the same **Time** knew that Cain *(Soul)* was the only one that could decide the final outcome of the situation.

No where in the first four chapters of Genesis will you find God telling mankind what to offer Him. Second, why should He? Able was presenting unto the LORD a sacrifice that met the LORD's approval. Third and lastly, Cain was a servant of **Sin**, an enemy of God, and against the Word of the LORD that said, "*if thou doest well, shalt thou not be accepted? and if thou doest not well, **Sin** lieth at the door*". Had Cain spent some **Time** meditating on this word, it would have kept him from **Sinning** against the Lord *(2Sam 12:1-13)* and killing his brother. Let's read *1 Cor 10:13*. It reads,

*"There hath no temptation taken you but such as is common to man: but **God is faithful, who will not suffer you to be tempted above that ye are able**; but will with the temptation also make a way to escape, that ye may be able to bear it."*

The Lord God had already spoken a word to Cain that would have made a way for him to escape the knowledge of *Sin* that was oppressing him and lying at the door of his heart blinding him from loving his brother. Look at verses 6 and 7. *Sin* was lying at the door. *Sin* lies at the door of our heart and soul all the *Time* waiting for us to open a doorway so that *Death* may enter and take somebody's life from them. Aah *Death*, what are you doing here in chapter 2? Go back to Chapter 5; it isn't *Time* to talk about you yet. So, in verse 8, *Sin* vexed Cain's soul until he became exceedingly angry at Abel and slew him. Not only did Cain fail to heed the advice of the LORD, he also violated the instructions given to us in *Eph 4:26*. Do you do this? Do you give *Sin* the *Time* it needs to *process* itself until it becomes exceedingly sinful *(Romans 7:13)*.

The Dictionary defines *process* as *"a continuing development involving many changes"*. This is the reason why people experience so many changes through out the day. In *Romans 7:5*, the Apostle Paul speaks about this *Sin* in our members, its continuous movement and its temptations which oppress us until we open a doorway for *Death* to enter our presence. This is another reason why men and women need to **hear** *Romans 10:17*, **receive** *John 1:12*, and **believe** *John 3:16*. For it is in God's Word, *Romans 12:21* that we read, *"Be not overcome of evil, but overcome evil with good"* and *1 Cor 9:27* that says *"But I keep under my body, and bring it into subjection: lest that by any means, when I have preached to others, I myself should be a castaway"*. When you hear verses like these *you need to receive, believe, and remember them.* Why? Because *Rev 12:12* tells us *the devil has a short **Time*** to persuade men to succumb to his temptations. Satan hears the Word of God being preached all over this wicked world. Yet, men and women are living as though they do not hear it, and failing to realize that *Time* is also running out on them. Let me illustrate.

While growing up in life, I found myself confronted with a lot of test put on me by men. Now, the most notable tests I remember are the SAT test for college enrollment and The Army Physical Fitness Test. These test made me nervous. What made me nervous about these test? These test were *Time*d. Man put a *Time* limit on how long I would be able take the test. I found myself at the mercy of *Time*. I needed *Time* to be on my side because when the allotted *Time* expired, the administrators stopped the test. After the *Time* ended, as far as they were concerned, I was finished whether I wanted to be or not. On that day, I was not allowed any retakes or restarts no matter if I passed or failed. Now, these are man-made rules. People who are made in God's own image created these rules. Now, if we who are made in God's own image do not believe in giving second chances, *then* on the Day of Judgment, what in the world makes you believe that the very image itself will act contrariwise? When a man or woman's *Time* on earth ends, they will depart this world, and like *Romans 14:12* promises, *every one of us shall give account of ourselves to God*. At the end of my SAT test, I had to give account. At the end of my Physical Fitness Test, I had to give account. At the end of my life on earth, I will have to give account. I hear your question, *"Minister Redd, what will I have to give an account for?"* Well, hear my question, *"How much* ***Time*** *in the day do you spend doing the will of the* ***Flesh*** *instead of the will of the father?"* *"How much* ***Time*** *in the day do you spend at the mall instead of at work?"* Do you think your boss would approve of this seeing that he is paying you based on the *Time* he thinks you have spent at work? Believers, when you previously walked *(Eph 2:2)* according to the lust of your *Flesh*, Satan was your master and he would tempt you with things that caused you to waste your *Time* and he has plans to keep us cumbered about with many things, just as he kept Martha in *Luke 10: 40-41* until our *Time* on earth expires and *Death* takes us out of this world.

Did you know that every second of every hour of every day can be spent ***in the presence of the LORD, doing the Father's will***? A life built on a solid foundation *(Matt 16:18)* with Christ as our life *(Col 3:4, Philippians 1:21)* in this world that lieth in wickedness. Yeah, that's right. A life capable of overcoming every temptation of Satan that our wretched earth suit as stated by Paul in *Romans 7:24* earnestly desires.

The Bible testifies about the life of two men, born of **Flesh** and blood just like you who overcame the **Sin** mingled in their earth suit. Their names are, Enoch and Elijah. Oh yes, and according to *1John 1:8,* they had **Sin**. No, Jesus is not one of them. Jesus, the last Adam *(1Cor 15:45)* was conceived of the Holy Ghost through the Virgin Mary to "*save us from our Sins*" *Matt 1:21*. In addition, *2 Cor. 5:21* says, "*For He* **(God)** *hath made Him* **(Jesus)** *to be Sin for us, who* **(Christ)** *knew no Sin; that we might be made the righteousness of God in Him* **(Christ)**.

Enoch and Elijah were born of human descendants but I will only address the life of Enoch. In *Genesis 5:21-24*, we read this testimony about his life,

"*And Enoch lived sixty and five years, and begat Methuselah: And Enoch walked with God after he begat Methuselah three hundred years, and begat sons and daughters: And all the days of Enoch were three hundred sixty and five years: And Enoch walked with God: and he was not; for God took him.*"

Enoch, a human, born of the **Flesh** of Adam, used his **Time** to walk with God until his mind, will, and emotions were so submitted to the Christ-life that *he was not; for God took him*. **That he was not what**? An unforgiver, a liar, an un-cheerful giver, or high-minded, but most importantly, he was a person who **lived according to the desires of his Flesh**. How did he do it? He used all his **Time** walking by faith that kept his mind stayed on what he heard the Word of God saying *(Romans 10:17)*. Enoch knew the value of **Time** spent in the presence of God whereas millions of humans **including myself at Times** do not. Furthermore, what makes Enoch's life even more outstanding is the **fact** that this man lived in his earth suit "*three hundred sixty and five years*" before God took him. Most humans' barely live *eighty years* before they die and some of them scarcely spend any *__Time__* talking or walking with the LORD.

The Bible even testifies of Jesus' Apostles going through periods where they wasted *__Time__* too. *Matt 16:15-16* tells us that Peter and the other Apostle's, who walked three and a half years with Jesus and knew He was the Christ wasted *__Time__* carrying out the Father's Will after Christ was crucified. When Christ's earth suit *(John 1:14, Jesus)* was crucified and descended on high, it took Christ *__Three Times__* to reveal himself as Jesus again to his disciples before they finally stopped wasting *__Time__*. Do you know what they were wasting *__Time__* doing the *__Third Time__* Christ appeared unto them? Look at what *John 21:3*, says,

"Simon Peter saith unto them, I go a __fishing__. They say unto him, __We also go with thee__. They went forth, and entered into a ship immediately; __and that night they caught nothing.__"

The same thing they were doing when the LORD first called them into ministry, *fishing, that's why they caught nothing* and a reason why many ministries are not enlarging. The sad thing about it is that in *John 20:22-23,* the second *__Time__* the LORD appeared unto them, He *__breathed__* on them the Holy Ghost, and told them what to do about the *__Sins__* of men. *__There He goes breathing again__* (Gen 2:7).

We like the disciples' waste too much *__Time__* living to the lust of our *__Flesh__* too. Living the life we lived *(Phil 3:13-16)* prior to entering our New Covenant relationship with Christ and there are many Christians who love to call themselves sanctified; which means "*to be set apart*". Set apart for what? So that you can continue to waste *__Time__* as you did before rebirth of the water and of the Spirit. The life lived by Enoch speaks against us all, now I see why God took him. His obedience and desire to spend *__Time__* walking with God prompted God to transform him out of *__Time__* and into eternity. When are we going to allow the word of God to transform us into the image of His Son?

Let me give you a better understanding of *Time*. God created the earth In *Time*. How do I know this? Look at *Genesis 1:1-2*, it says,

> *"In the beginning God created the heaven and the earth. And the earth was without form, and void; and darkness was upon the face of the deep. And the Spirit of God moved upon the face of the waters."*

There is nothing written in these verses which indicate that Heaven was without form or void. Heaven was formed and filled with spiritual life. Heaven is where God dwells, it is a spiritual place; a place of eternity. It was the Earth that needed to be formed and inhabited and before God created our world, *Time* did not exist. So, in *Genesis 1:2-31*, God begins to create things, and He creates by days (*there is no such thing as days in eternity, eternity is timeless, dayless*). God calls the mornings and the evening's day *verse 5* but calls darkness night *verse 4*. *John 3:19* says that men love darkness more than light. God hates darkness. Why? Darkness hinders a person from beholding the Glory of God's creation. A blind person lives their entire life in darkness unable to behold anything; This has never been God will for anyone. Was the first man Adam created blind? Therefore, God separated darkness from the day. This separation of darkness from the day is how we make up the three separate *Times* of a 24 hour day (*morning-evening-night*). God calls day good, *verse 4* but never mentions night. Men therefore, took these days and divided them into *seconds, minutes, and hours* and probably believe days are without end but the *day of the Lord* will end our days *(2Peter 3:10)*. Now, *seconds, minutes and hours* are components of *Time* so let me give you an illustration of how *Time* works against us.

Time is what a farmer gives to his chickens living on his farm. Let's say this farmer keeps his chickens in a barn until the *Time* comes for him to cook a meal made of chicken. Do you think he *Cares* about which chicken he kills to enjoy his meal? No, his mind is made up; he wants chicken for his meal. I feel sorry for the chicken he chooses because that chicken's life will be required in order for the farmers desire to be met and there is nothing that chicken can do to escape the farmer's desire, nothing. That chicken now finds itself in a **Dilemma**.

The first man Adam placed all men in a **Dilemma** like this chicken. The barn is **Time**, our earth suit is the Chicken, and our soul *(Container)* is what the LORD desires, who is also the farmer and look at what He says to us in *Ezekiel 18:4*,

"*Behold, **all souls are mine**; as the soul of the father, so also the soul of the son is mine: **the soul that sinneth, it shall die**.*"

Now, what did the chicken do to deserve **Death**? Nothing. What have you and I done to deserve **Death**? Be born in an earth suit. ***Why do we have to die***? Because our earth suit is a *body of **Sin*** and the vehicle Satan uses to keep us disbelieving and rebelling against the Word of God *(John 1:1, 14)*. Let's read *Romans 5:12,*

"*Wherefore, as by one man sin entered into the world, and death by sin; and so death passed upon all men, for that **all have sinned**.*"

According to this verse, ***all have sinned***. How does a person know when they are sinning? Look at "*How much **Time** in a day you spend fulfilling the lust of the flesh instead of the will of the father?*" "*How much **Time** in the day do you spend walking with God versus your enjoyment of living in this world with all its lust?* When the **Time** arrives, will the Lord say unto you, "*Well done, thou good and faithful servant: thou hast been faithful over a few things, I will make thee ruler over many things: enter thou into the joy of thy lord*" *(Matt 25:21-23)*. Let's pray that He does. Or will He profess, "*I never knew you: depart from me, ye that work iniquity *(Matthew 7:23)*.

When the first man Adam faced the test of obeying or disobeying the *sayings and teachings of the LORD God*, he was not in life, *the breathe of life was in them (Gen 2:7)* but he wasn't

28

in **Death** either. Instead of making mankind like robots, the LORD God let the first man Adam and Eve make the choice of which life they wanted for themselves and their offspring to live in. The first Adam was given two choices and one of the choices came with a warning. The last Adam, the lamb who was slain before the foundation of the world, as revealed in _Rev 13:8_, counseled the first man Adam on the dangers associated with the Tree of the Knowledge of Good and Evil and about **Death** in case the first man Adam partook of it. It was a test of devotion. A devotion to worship Him in spirit and in truth or die. So, according to _John 4:23_, all God ever wanted from mankind was for us to worship Him in Spirit and in Truth. Nothing else created by God would reveal to God how much the first man Adam truly loved and worshipped Him other than the decision he would make concerning these two trees in the Garden of Eden.

The first man Adam willfully chose **Death** over life. **_That is why you and I have to die_**. The first man Adam's disobedience passed **Death** upon all men and all men have an appointment with **Death** according to _Heb 9:27_. When a person gets an appointment, they also are given a **_Time_** for that appointment. But, in the game of life, a **_Time_** is not given, only a warning. Look at what _Job 7:1 and Luke 12:16-21_ says. They say,

"**_Is there not an appointed Time to man upon earth_**? _are not his days also like the days of an hireling?_"

"_And he spake a parable unto them, saying, The ground of a certain rich man brought forth plentifully: And **he thought within himself**, saying, What shall I do, because I have no room where to bestow my fruits? And he said, This will I do: I will pull down my barns, and build greater; and there will I bestow all my fruits and my goods. And I will say to my soul, Soul, thou hast much goods laid up for many years; take thine ease, eat, drink, and be merry. But **God said unto him, Thou fool**, this night thy soul shall be required of thee: then whose shall those things be,_ *which thou hast provided? So is he that layeth up treasure for himself, and is not rich toward God"*

Notice, it was God, not the LORD God who called this man a fool? Why? *Proverbs 24:9* says, *"The thought of foolishness is **Sin**"* and *Psalms 14:1* says, *"The fool hath said in his heart, There is no God"*. This man had foolish thoughts. Do you have foolish thoughts? Job's wife did *(Job 2:9-10)*. Secondly, this man does not have the power to determine whether he lives another ***day*** or not *(John 19:10-11)*. Also of importance is the ***fact*** that this man never acknowledged or reverenced God for any of the blessings he had received throughout his life. Let's read *Psalms 23:6*. It says,

*"Surely <u>goodness and mercy shall follow me **all** the days of my life</u>: and I will **dwell in the house of the Lord** for ever."*

These are the words of a worshipper, Praise God. According to this verse, how many ***days*** shall goodness and mercy follow us? **All** of them. Does this verse address after-life? No, but the Word of God does in *Hebrews 9:27*. How many of his days do you think this farmer used to seek after the Kingdom of God *(Matt 6:33)* or to spend ***Time*** with Him? None, he spent his ***Time*** thinking within himself about how easier he could make his life on this earth for his soul when he should have been praying, " *Lord, make me to know mine end, and the measure of my days, what it is; that I may know how frail I am. Behold, thou hast made my days as an handbreadth; and mine age is as nothing before thee: verily every man at his best state is altogether vanity. Selah. Surely every man walketh in a vain shew: surely they are disquieted in vain: <u>he heapeth up riches, and knoweth not who shall gather them</u>. And now, Lord, what wait I for? my hope is in thee. Deliver me from all my transgressions: make me not the reproach of the foolish." (Psalms 39:4-8)*

How much ***Time*** did he ***dwell in the house of the Lord***? Not his house, the house of the Lord. I don't see any from these verses. There are too many humans, born again believers too, who have similar thoughts like this man; thoughts that keep them from realizing that during their *Time* of selfishness, **Sin** had been processing a way for **Death** to take them out of this world.

We humans are very familiar with the process of *Time*. We are governed by *Time*. Remember my story about the SAT test and the Army Physical Fitness Test. We schedule our appointments by *Time*, we arrive and depart from certain locations by *Time*, and feel lost when we do not know the *Time*. Yet, the most important thing millions of humans never think about is the *Time* they will die. For if men and women thought more about the *Time* they will die, they would seek after God more diligently. Humans must learn to live with eternity in view, not with the temporal things of this world in view. It is imperative that we mortify our earth suits with all its passions before we die because whether we do or don't, all **Flesh** will return unto the dust of the Earth as written in *Job 34:15 and Gen 3:19*. Guess what it is that makes humans think like that rich man mentioned in *Luke 12:16-21*? Let's read *Proverbs 19:21*. It says,

"There are many devices (ideas, plans) in a man's heart; nevertheless the counsel of the LORD, that shall stand."

Mingled and living *(Romans 7:23)* inside our earth suit *(Jer 17:9)* is a nature that oppresses men to make all kinds of plans but seldomly will you find many setting aside *Time* to commune with God. They have more pressing matters to *Care* about. Just look at the lifestyle they live. In this decade, mankind makes so many plans and these plans have driven them to create a book known as an Organizer, a small computer known as a Palm Pilot, and an even better compact computer-organizer known as a Blackberry. These three things are used for scheduling appointments, dinner dates, vacations, etc. They are devices invented in *Time* to record events that men and women have planned for future engagements but I'll bet you will hardly find anything recorded in these devices confirming that they have set aside any *Time* to commune with God. Satan, the god of this world assisted men with the creation of these devices so that men would be able to better organize the things that keep men cumbered about and blind to the message of the Gospel. Why? It gives Satan the **_Time_** he needs to process a plan using the **_Sin_** contained in their hearts to delay them from receiving the spiritual rebirth men need before their **_Time_** on Earth expires. Some believers are no different. Look at the way professing Christians are living. There are professing Christian brothers and sisters today who say they have a relationship with the LORD but have plans to commit adultery on their marriage partner this week, *they know who they are*. There are professing Christians all in the workplace today who have plans to steal from their employers, *they know who they are*. Steal what? **_Time_**. Not physical items. They can be replaced. **_Time_** cannot. What do you do when you go to work? There are Professing Christians today who have plans to bear false witness against their neighbor, *they know who they are* and I hope that what the Holy Spirit is revealing through this book halts them *(2Cor 10:3-5)*. Halts them from what? From yielding to the lust of the **_Flesh_** caused by the motions of **_Sin_** at work in their self-proclaimed crucified bodies. **Yes, _self-proclaimed_** and the only way Sin is able to do this is because these believers have not **_truly_** taken the **_Time_** to seriously mortify their earth suit as instructed in *Colossians 3:5*, nor have they put any effort *(1Tim 6:12)* into staying submitted to the instructions given by James in *James 1:22 and 4:7*. Their failure to do this opens a doorway for unclean spirits to gain entrance back into their life as mentioned in *Luke 11:24-26*.

I know there is someone who doesn't believe what I have written. However, I do not **_Care_** if you do not believe what I have written. It's your **_Dilemma_**; I have been anointed to shed the light of God's Word, mentioned in *John 1:5*, on your **_Dilemma_**. Christ has commissioned me to do it and I will carry out this commission *(Matt 10:12-20)*.

Martha was a believer yet *Luke 10:40-42* tells us that she was running around doing the wrong thing with her **_Time_**, while the LORD was speaking the Word of life in **_her house_**. Likewise, many humans are either busy trying to please others, too busy enjoying life, or enjoying what they think is life, while

Sin is steadily processing a storm for them and because they haven't taken the ***Time*** to deny themselves and live the Christ-life mentioned in *Phil 2:5 (believers, look at Luke 9:62)*. These people will never see the Kingdom of God. Let's read *Matthew 7: 24-28*. They read,

> *"Therefore **whosoever heareth these sayings of mine, and doeth them, I will liken him unto a wise man,** which built his house upon a rock: And the rain descended, and the floods came, and the winds blew, and beat upon that house; and it fell not: for it was founded upon a rock. And **every one that heareth these sayings of mine, and doeth them not, shall be likened unto a foolish man**, which built his house upon the sand: And the rain descended, and the floods came, and the winds blew, and beat upon that house; and it fell: and great was the fall of it.*

Many humans today, even though they have heard this teaching repeatedly, continue to build their lifestyle upon sand *(the flesh)* which is exactly what our earth suit is made of as declared in *Genesis 2:7, 3:19*.

Let's look at the book of Ecclesiastes. *Ecclesiastes 3: 1-9*, but I want to teach it in reverse, verses 9-1.

Verse 9 says, *"What profit hath he that worketh in that wherein he laboureth?"*

Humans spend most of their ***Time*** doing labor. Labor means *"to work"*. In order to make a means for living in this world, We have to work. We do this work based on a ***Time*** system. However, when it pertains to the work of God, the only work men are told to do is *"believe on the one whom God has sent"* spoken by Jesus himself in *John 6:27-29*. Humans now are told that our labor is the believing of God's Word. The Word ministered by Jesus and His disciple's to the new creature in Christ *(2Cor 5:17)*, not the words we have been hearing from worldly leaders, including the religious ones living contrary to the Word of God *(Psalms 1:1)*. Especially some the ones who *begin their name with Reverend*.

Let's revisit the man in *Luke 12:16-21* who wasted ***Time*** enjoying life to the lust of his ***Flesh***. Again, it reads,

> *And he spake a parable unto them, saying, the ground of a certain rich man brought forth plentifully: And he thought within himself, saying, what shall I do, because I have no room where to bestow my fruits? And he said, this will I do: I will pull down my barns, and build greater; and there will I bestow all my fruits and my goods. And I will say to my soul, Soul, thou hast much goods laid up for many years* (he thinks he has a lot of time); *take thine ease, eat, drink, and be merry.* <u>*But God said unto him, Thou fool, this **night** thy soul shall be required of thee: then whose shall those things be, which thou hast provided?*</u> *So is he that layeth up treasure for himself, and is not rich toward God.*

Notice I highlighted the word, ***night***. In Genesis, Chapter one, God separated the ***day*** from the night. Separation does not mean ending. Webster's dictionary defines separation as, "*A point, line, or means of division*". Look at what God did in *Genesis 1:4*. This verse says,

> "*And God saw the light, that it was good: and **God divided** the light from the darkness.*"

Division does not end, it separates. This certain rich man spent the majority of his ***Time*** living in the night. Why did I say that? *Well, why didn't God talk to him in the day*? Do you spend a lot of ***Time*** living your life in darkness? I am sure this man heard somebody preaching the Word of God at some ***Time*** in his life. The Bible proclaims that Noah preached to everyone in his ***day***. Still, only he and his family survived the flood. It's sad when God has to come into the ***night*** to tell a man or woman something because they love darkness *(John 3:19)* so much that neither God nor a preacher *(Rom 10:14)* can get them to come into the light *(day)* of God's Word. Do you spend most of your ***Time*** in the night *(In Sin)*? I sure hope not, because there is coming a ***Time*** in every human's life that ***Death*** will require of them their soul.

Have you been displaying a lifestyle resembling that of this certain rich man? I sure hope not, but if you have, my prayer is that you will allow the Word of God to *call you out of darkness and into his marvelous light: which in **Times** past were not a people, but are now the people of God (1Peter 2:9-10)*. Let's look at *Galatians 6:7-8*, they read,

*"Be not deceived; God is not mocked: for whatsoever a man soweth, that shall he also reap. For he that soweth to his flesh shall of the flesh reap corruption; but he that **soweth to the Spirit shall of the Spirit reap life everlasting.**"*

Please, set aside some ***Time*** during the ***day*** and to allow the Word of God to be sown into your life and follow Peter's advice given in *Acts 2:38*. Again, please look at this certain rich man's mindset. He had not given heed to the things of the Spirit concerning the verses from Acts, Romans, or *1Tim 6:6-10* and when his appointed ***Time*** with ***Death*** arrived, I am sure he was sorrowful after hearing the voice of God and realizing that he had not obtained any of the treasures mentioned in *2Cor 4: 7-10* that could have saved him from eternal damnation as stated in *Mark 16:16*. Have you made Jesus Christ your foundation? Have you been building *(Laboring)* with your faith while living on this earth in ***Time***.

Verse 8 through 2 speaks on this wise,

*(8) "A time to love, and a time to hate; a time of war, and a time of peace. (7)A time to rend, and a time to sew; a time to keep silence, and a time to speak. (6) A time to get, and a time to lose; a time to keep, and a time to cast away. (5) A time to cast away stones, and a time to gather stones together; a time to embrace, and a time to refrain from embracing. (4) A time to weep, and a time to laugh; a time to mourn, and a time to dance. (3) A time to kill, and a time to heal; a time to break down, and a time to build up. (2) A time to be born, **and a time to die;** a time to plant, and a time to pluck up that which is planted.*

I am forty-two years old and as I read through those verses of scripture, one thing came to mind. There has been a **_Time_** in my life that I've experienced everything written in those verses except for one thing, **_physical death_**. Why? My appointed **_Time_** with **Death** hasn't arrived yet. When will it arrive? I do not know but I know my **Flesh** will experience corruption. Why? Because _Genesis 3:19_ says so and because it is _the Body of Sin_; a body that bringeth forth **Death**.

Let's look at **_Time_** from a different view. _Romans 13:11-14_ says,

"_And that, knowing the **Time**, that now it is high **Time** to awake out of sleep (spiritual death) for now is our salvation nearer than when we believed. The **night** is far spent, the **day** is at hand: let us therefore cast off the works of **darkness**, and let us put on the armour of **light**. Let us walk honestly, as in the **day**; not in rioting and drunkenness, not in chambering and wantonness, not in strife and envying. But **put ye on the Lord Jesus Christ, and make not provision for the flesh, to fulfil the lusts thereof**._

My **Flesh** has an appointed **_Time_** with **Death**. There is coming a day that Roderick Redd as well as yourself, will embrace **Death** in our earthen vessels prior to Christ's return to earth or **_when He arrives_** as stated in _Matt 16:28._ Therefore, because I know this **day** exists, my **Flesh** trembles. On the other hand, thanks to the **Death** of Jesus on the cross and the words of _Hebrews 2:14-15_, my soul is at peace. These words are,

"_Forasmuch then as the children are partakers of flesh and blood, he **(Jesus)** also himself likewise took part of the same; that **through death** he might destroy him that had the power of death, that is, the devil; and **deliver them who through fear of death** were all their lifetime subject to bondage_".

The washing of regeneration and renewing of the Holy Ghost _(Titus 3:4)_ empowered my born again life to where it cannot die nor is it affected by **_Time_**. Any man, male or female who does not believe what I just wrote and fail to **believe** in the name of Jesus and receive Christ as their life before their **Flesh's** appointed **Time** to die, will be judged as written in *Rev 20: 11-15*. For if we do not call upon the name of the Lord, we make *it impossible* for our soul to be saved as promised in *St.John 3:16-18 / Mark 16:16 / Acts 2:21*.

Verse 1 speaks on this wise,

"*To every thing there is a season, and a **Time** to every purpose **under** the heaven.*"

Time, exist **under** heaven. Heaven is a spiritual place where God, the man Christ Jesus who ascended into Heaven in *Acts 1:9-11*, and obedient angels live. It is a place not affected by **Time** because Heaven is a spiritual world and those who live there are spirit *(John 4:24, Psalms 104:4, Hebrews 1:7)*. However, the Word of God testifies in *Revelations 21:1* that this Heaven will pass away with the Earth at the end of **Time**. So, stop putting your dead and buried loved ones in a place that God never intended for mankind to abide. The Bible says in *2Cor 5:17-19,* that our loved ones who have died and gone are in Christ. Therefore, leave them in Christ until the new Heaven in *Rev 21:1* appears. Nevertheless, they will not be there either. They'll live on the new Earth. No where in the Bible does it say that when men die they go to Heaven. However, *Eccles. 3:21* does say, "*Who knoweth **the spirit of man** that goeth upward, and the spirit of the beast that goeth downward to the earth?*" **Man is a soul** and his spirit goes upward after **Death** because that is where it came from. Man's spirit is the Breathe of Life.

Now, *Eph 2:6* does say that Christ has made us to sit together in **_heavenly places_**, *not in heaven*. The Garden of Eden was a heavenly place. So, if we believe that God and Angels exist, then we have to include the Garden of Eden in our belief. Before the first man Adam and Eve sinned, the Garden of Eden was where the first man Adam and Eve made their abode. I personally **believe** that men and women who die in Christ either go here or they are sleeping in Christ. *Genesis 3:24* says, "The

Garden of Eden existed with *Cherubims and a flaming sword which turned every way keeping the way of the tree of life".* That verse signifies that the Garden of Eden exists. However, only Spiritual beings are permitted to dwell there. The first man Adam and Eve prior to **Sinning**, were present with the LORD God in the Garden of Eden possessing no carnal knowledge. Furthermore, Paul in *2 Cor. 5:8-9* says, *"We are confident, I say, and willing rather to be **absent from the body, and to be present with the Lord. Wherefore we labour**, that, whether present or absent, we may be accepted of him.* At the beginning of **Time**, the first man Adam and Eve's mind was spiritual and without any knowledge of their earth suit. Guess where they were during this **Time**? They were in the Garden of Eden and now that Christ has restored believers back to the Father's original mindset from the beginning, *"Where do you think He restores us to when we are absent from our earthen vessels"?* Not Heaven. In the beginning, men were created to have dominion over the earth. The Garden of Eden was created on the earth and is still on this planet. We just cannot see it. Why? I believe the reason we cannot see it is because the Garden of Eden is located in the Light/day. This world we live in is the Night/darkness. Remember, God separated the day from the night. When you die, if you are walking in the light, I believe you will reenter the Garden of Eden at the conclusion of your earth suit's life in this world. So, stop putting humans in Heaven. Leave them in Christ or put them in the Garden of Eden. Heaven is a place where God, the man Christ Jesus who ascended into Heaven in *Acts 1:9-11*, and obedient angels live, not humans.

Now, Satan and the third of the angels who were disobedient as mentioned in *Jude 6* who kept not their first **Estate** *(heaven)* are prisoned in **Hell** until the end of **Time** and on Judgment Day, they will be cast into a lake of fire as written in *Rev 20:10, 14-15.*

Now, Webster's dictionary defines the word "**Estate**" as land. What is land? Heaven was the land these angels once lived in, a place of eternity, a place inhabited by spiritual beings. The earth also is land. Yet many of us fail to keep our **dust of the** *earth formed vessels* under subjection to the Word of God just like these spiritual beings failed to keep theirs. Why? The first man Adam's one season of *Sin* imprisoned Satan, those fallen angels and all of humanity in an earthen vessel in *Time* and *Death* is the only way to depart it but spirits can't die. Furthermore, when they rebelled against God, they did it in Eternity *(Rev 12:12, Luke 10:18)*. Thanks be unto God, *Adam rebelled in Time, not in eternity.* Nevertheless, *Eph 2:8 and John 14:6* tells us that the grace of God made a way for believers to translate *(Col 1:13-14)* out of *Time* and overcome the sting of *Death (1Cor 15:55)* by sending his only begotten son, Jesus Christ *into Time* to delivered us from the power of darkness *(Col 1:13-14)* before our appointment with *Death*.

Did you know that *Death* is the tool God uses to translate men out of *Time* and into eternity? The problem with humans *and many believers* is that we have not come to realize the importance of the message in *Philippians 2:7-8*, a message of when Christ Jesus *took upon himself the form of a servant, made in the likeness of men, and humbled himself, becoming obedient unto Death, even the Death of the Cross* to save men and imprison Satan in an earth suit. Why did God want to imprison Satan in an earth suit? Satan was an angel. Angels were created as spirits, not creatures of the earth. But the mystery of God that neither Satan nor ninety percent of our church leaders know is that when the first man Adam ate of that forbidden tree, Not only did Satan cause the first man Adam to fall but imprisoned himself and his evil nature in man's formed earth suit. A suit prepared by the Lord God in *Genesis 2:7* probably for that purpose yet unrevealed to men and hidden from Satan. Today, the difference between men and Satan is that God promises men that they will be saved in the day of His wrath if they believe in His son. However, God never promised this to Satan or to the other fallen Angels although they *believe* and know who Jesus is *(James 2:19)*. Still, millions of human beings do not *believe* in God's promises and this unbelief eliminates any chance of them escaping God's soon coming judgment on this world.

The Bible plainly teaches that the world we live in is surrounded by darkness and the way to get out of this darkness is found in *John 3: 3 & 5*. These verses read,

*"Jesus answered and said unto him, Verily, verily, I say unto thee, except a man be born again, he cannot see the kingdom of God"; **and** "Jesus answered, Verily, verily, I say unto thee, except a man be born of water and of the Spirit, he cannot enter into the kingdom of God."*

Some people, after having read or heard these verses, still continue to spend the majority of their *Time* obeying the lust of their *Flesh* due to Satan's oppressive temptations but these temptations are no different than the ones he tempted Jesus with in *Matthew 4:1-11*. Some believers today also, have been displaying before the world and heaven a lifestyle resembling that of the first man Adam and Eve, who themselves chose not to spend *Time* enjoying their fellowship with the Lord but decided to spend *Time* conversating with the Devil, disguised as a serpent *(Rev 20:2)*. What disguise is Satan using on you? Don't let Satan dominate your thoughts with his temptations.

Remember, Satan has been judged and condemned to spend eternity in the lake of fire. Humans have been judged to die but are given the choice *(Josh 24:15)* of determining where we shall spend eternity. Say this prayer with me,

*"Lord, I thank you for the interval of Time and the longsuffering you grant to me every day of my life. Lord, please strengthen me in my God created spirit man to deny myself, take up my cross and follow you. I now realize the value of **Time** and desire to redeem it so that I may give you all the glory, all the honor, and all the praise that you deserve. If Enoch can do it, so can I. In Jesus name I pray, Amen.*

Care

But he turned, and said unto Peter, Get thee behind me, Satan: thou art an offence unto me: <u>for thou savourest (Carest) not the things that be of God, but those that be of men.</u>
Matthew 16:23

Care. Yes, **Care**. <u>*Romans 5:12*</u> tells us that the first Adam's disobedience passed a nature upon all men. A nature that has made all men sinners and come short of the glory of God. Wherefore, God cursed every man and woman in <u>*Gen 3:16-19*</u> and placed demands on them *(Laws and ordinances Col 2:14)*. These demands were not placed on men for them to keep but to show them how sinful they were and their need for a Saviour. Nevertheless, men to this day including some church leaders are ignorant of this *fact* and zealously <u>*(Romans 10:2)*</u> attempt to live by laws. Notice, I said attempt. Many seem to **Care** about nothing but submitting themselves to laws and ordinances. Ordinances and laws that <u>*Col. 2:23*</u> says, "*Which things have indeed a shew of wisdom in will worship, and humility, and neglecting of the body; not in any honour to the satisfying of the flesh.*" But they cannot save men's souls from **Death**. Something men **Care** much about whether they acknowledge it or not.

Now, Webster's Dictionary defines **Care** as, "*a troubled state of mind; to worry*" but I would like to define **Care** as "*an oppression of the mind weighed down by responsibilities*". Spiritually speaking, I would define it as "<u>*the troubling of a human's soul to propel it to react*</u>" and this troubling is utilized by God and the Devil. However, in <u>*Matthew 4:1-10*</u>, we read that the **Christ-life** in Jesus withstood the oppression applied to it by the Devil and the major reason why born-again believers are instructed in <u>*Philippians 2:5*</u> to "*Let this mind be in you, which was also in Christ Jesus*" because only the **Christ-Life Mind** has been able to the Devil's oppressive attacks placed upon it. Christ did not **Care** for anything the Devil offered Him during that **Time** of temptation in the wilderness. His mind had one desire.

41

A desire that wanted nothing but to please the Father *(Heb 11:6)*. The Devil knew this but used every temptation he could to entice Jesus into submitting to the *__Cares__* of his **Flesh** *(Matt 4:1-11)* above doing the Will of the Father and pleasing Him. Today, Satan continues to utilize these same tactics on born again believers and he does it through those areas of their life which they *__Care__* the most about. But, the Apostle Paul being instructed by the Holy Spirit in *Galatians 5:16-18* has these words for us. He says,

*"This I say then, Walk in the Spirit, and ye shall not fulfil the lust of the flesh. For the flesh lusteth against the Spirit, and the Spirit against the flesh: and these are contrary the one to the other: so that ye cannot do the things that ye would. **But if ye be led of the Spirit, ye are not under the law**."*

Whoever the Devil finds walking in the Spirit, he will attack. How will he attack? He'll attack you through the weaknesses/***__Cares__*** of your **Flesh**. He will attack you until the lustful desires of your **Flesh** is to overbearing for you to resist them *(James 4:7)*. He used this very tactic In the life of Job. Read Job, chapters 1 and 2. Satan tempted Job with a heavy burden, but Job had a sound mind *(2Tim 1:7)*. A mind unfazed by Satanic attacks. Satanic attacks that the Devil knows a true worshipper of God walking in the Spirit does not let worry them to much.

Now, I need for you to please pay close attention to the conclusion of verse 18. It reads, "***But if ye be led of the Spirit, ye are not under the law***". The word Law mentioned in this verse is not referring to the Law of Moses. Why do I say this? Because the writer is addressing Romans; Romans are Gentiles and were a law unto themselves *(Rom 2:14)*. They were people whom Moses never gave the law *(Romans 2:14)*. However, if he were addressing the Nation of Israel, the meaning would remain the same because the Law of God could not deliver them from the power of **Sin**. Why? It was made weak through the lust of their **Flesh**. All you have to do is ask Samson and King David.

*"For what **the law** could not <u>do, in</u> <u>that</u> it **was weak through the flesh,** God sending his <u>own</u> <u>Son</u> in the <u>likeness</u> of <u>sinful flesh, and for sin, condemned sin in</u> the flesh".*

The law received by Moses and given to the Israelites was weak when it came to condemning the **Sin** nature in their earth suit passed. Now, <u>Romans 7:12</u> does tell us that the Law received by Moses is spiritual and good. However, it is made weak through the **Flesh**. I did not say this, <u>Romans 8:3</u> said it, I am only expounding on that verse. The Old Testament testifies of men and women who lived <u>before the law</u> was given (*Esau, Joseph's Brothers*) and <u>under the law</u> *(Samson, King Saul, King David)* but the **Sin** that dwelt within their earth suit burdened them to such an extent that the Law was made of non effect because of the things they **_Cared_** about. The Law cannot deliver you from doing evil works nor will it help you, and this is the reason why we must come from under the law and let the Spirit lead us. Let's read *2 Tim. 4:18*, it says,

"And the Lord shall deliver me from every evil work, and will preserve me unto his heavenly kingdom: to whom be glory for ever and ever. Amen."

No matter how hard you try to live according to the law, it will not deliver you from Satan's persistent attacks. The Israelites, a nation God put under the Law *(Gal 4:4)*, had a King named David. Yet, in *2Sam 11:2-27*, it is evident that King David **_Cared_** more for himself and the wife of Uriah the Hittite being exposed for transgressing the Law than he **_Cared_** about the keeping of the law *(Romans 3:19)* or one of the Commandments. So, rather than having their **Sin** exposed, he had Uriah killed. King David **_Cared_** more for Bathsheba and personally saw to it that nothing would expose the evil adulterous deed they had committed with each other. Let's look at *John 8:3-5* and see why King David behaved himself in this manner and the judgment that awaited Bathsheba.

"And the scribes and Pharisees brought unto him a woman taken in adultery; and when they had set her in the midst,

They say unto him, Master, this woman was taken in adultery, in the very act. **Now Moses in the law commanded us, that such should be stoned:** *but what sayest thou?"*

King David knew the Law and the justice it demanded for anyone caught in Adultery. Yet, he **Cared** more for her than the Law or obeying *the sayings and teachings* of the Lord. Only **Sin** could make King David do this and some of us as well. Let's look at the Disciples of Christ again. Not only did they waste **Time**, but the Bible shows that for a period of **Time**, they did not **Care** *(the Spiritual troubling of a born-again believer's mind which causes the believer to go forth in the Word)* for the things of God when it came to doing the Will of the Father. In *John 20:23* after Jesus was crucified, buried, and had risen from the dead, He visited His disciples twice and gave them specific instructions concerning the souls of men. What did they do after receiving these instructions? According to *John 21:3,* they went fishing. Well, they should have been **Care**-ing for every human whose **Sin**s had not been remitted. Now, *John 20:22* says that the Lord had already breathed the Holy Ghost on them, which gave them the empowerment to carry out the Father's will for mankind but look at what they were doing with this empowerment *(anointing)*. Fishing and unless you and I take the **Time** to mortify the lust of our **Flesh**, **Sin** will hinder us from doing the Will of the Father and cause us to lust after certain things that have absolutely nothing to do with the Father's Will just as the disciples did.

Webster's Dictionary defines **lust** as "a *craving, a desiring*". It is **Care**-ing for something or someone we love. The disciples after having received Christ-given instructions in *John 20:22* did not lust after the spiritual **Care** that Christ and the Father desired for them to have concerning mankind and their desire to see men's **Sin**s remitted or retained. Please notice that this was the third **Time** Christ visited His disciples and Peter was present each **Time**. Can you now see why Christ in *John 21:17* asked Peter if he loved Him three **Times**? What did these three questions do to Peter? It grieved him. To grieve means *to trouble or burden.* Christ put spiritual **Care** on Peter with those three questions. Why? Because Christ was tired of Peter hearing and receiving Word of God, but failing to do what the Father desired him to do. *Matt 16:16-18* tells us that if there was anybody who knew who Christ was and what the Spirit was saying, was Peter. Nevertheless, the words from Peter's mouth truly revealed what Peter **Care**-d for. Let's read *Matt 16:21-23.* They read,

> "*From that time forth began Jesus to shew unto his disciples, how that he must go unto Jerusalem, and suffer many things of the elders and chief priests and scribes, and be killed, and be raised again the third day. Then Peter took him, and began to rebuke him, saying, Be it far from thee, Lord: this shall not be unto thee. But he turned, and said unto Peter, Get thee behind me, Satan: thou art an offence unto me: **for thou savourest not the things that be of God, but those that be of men**.*"

Jesus rebuked the **Sin** (*Satanic burdening of a believer's mind that causes him/her to **Care***) in Peter's earth suit because Jesus knew that it was Satan burdening Peter's soul and caused Peter to speak such words. Peter did not want Jesus to *suffer many things of the elders and chief priests and scribes, and be killed*, but in order for the Father's desire to be satisfied and for men to be saved, Jesus had to *suffer many things of the elders and chief priests and scribes, and be killed, and be raised again the third day.*

The **Sin** nature mingled in our **Flesh**, tempts us to *worry/care* about everything except the Will of God being done in a person's life, especially the ones we dislike. This worrying is most likely due to the **fact** that many believers, including myself at **Times**, are not spending enough **Time** in the Word of God seeking for a Word that'll strengthen us in our inner man until we are able to overcome the *Satanic burdening* on our soul to obey the Lord's commandments.

If you were to look at the outward lifestyle *(2Tim 3:1-7)* of most humans, you'll see that they either **Care** about

45

themselves, those they have a close relationship with *(family),* or someone that walks in agreement with them pertaining to each others *Flesh*-ly lust. They do not *Care* if you tell them not to lay on sandy beaches half-naked under the sun, but they *worry/care* about having skin cancer that comes from over exposure of the sun's rays to the body. They prefer to listen to educated liars who tell them that if they'll use sun tan lotion with the right protection, it will protect them from the sun's rays *(Psalms 1:1)*. Many people do not *Care* about the warnings associated with sex or using drugs, but they *worry/care* about HIV and AIDS, or being caught by law enforcement agents for selling drugs. Do you get the picture? Let me use myself for an example once again *(1Cor 9:27)*. Remember, no matter who you are, everyday brings with it *Care*s that you might find yourself confronted with.

I received a phone call from my sister about my niece, who went to go live with her stepmother, who so happened to live one hour and twenty minutes from the Army base I was stationed at. Her stepmother *(my niece said)* was not giving her any food to eat. I therefore felt *Care* (*a burdening of my mind that caused me to worry about my niece*) for my niece who I love fervently. I went and visited her, took her out to eat, and gave her some money. I did not have that much money but my *Care* for her overshadowed my needs and my love for her motivated me to sacrifice my needs to fulfil hers. After my *Care* (worry) for her was resolved, I departed. As I began to drive home, I heard the voice of the LORD say to me, "*I wish you would Care for the advancement of the Gospel the way you Care for your family*". I replied, "*Yes Lord, I now understand your teachings from Hebrews 12:5-11.*" The LORD said, "*Would you have given that much money to your pastor if he would have asked members to make a sacrificial offering for a need in the ministry?*" My answer was one of sorrow because God knew just as I knew that I would not have given it.

God can't be fooled, *Hebrews 4:12* tells us that God knows the thoughts and intents of the heart. Oh, I'll bet some of you church leaders liked that, but we have *some* church leaders who are worse than the members. The LORD has a few things to minister to you about this as well. One of the main reasons why there is a lack of spiritual **_Care_** in the body *(church)* today is the wastefulness of finances received during church services. Now, in *Ephesians 4:11-14*, the Bible says,

> "*And he gave **some**, apostles; and some, prophets; and some, evangelists; and some, pastors and teachers;* For the perfecting of the saints, for the work of the ministry, for the edifying of the body of Christ: Till we all come in the unity of the faith, and of the knowledge of the Son of God, unto a perfect man, unto the measure of the stature of the fulness of Christ: That we henceforth be no more children, tossed to and fro, and carried about with every wind of doctrine, by the sleight of men, and cunning craftiness, whereby they lie in wait to deceive.*"

It would be great if these leaders had a good understanding of what *Matt 6:34* really meant. Why? Because **_The Church Leadership_** is mostly responsible for believers not being able to overcome the **_Care_**s of this world. Now, *Ephesians 4* says that it was Our Lord and Saviour Jesus Christ who gave us our church leaders. However, **_some_** of our church leaders make it hard to believe that Christ would give the church **apostles; and _some_, prophets; and _some_, evangelists; and _some_, pastors and teachers** judging by the way they live. For we have **_some_** living as though they do not **_Care_** for their members more than the advancement of **_their ministry_**. Notice, I said **_their ministry_**. Let's look at *Matthew 13:22*, it says,

> "*He also that received seed among the thorns is he that heareth the word; and the **care** of this world, and the deceitfulness of riches, choke the word, and he becometh unfruitful.*"

I am the pastor of Christ Our Life Ministries in Augusta, Georgia. One day God sowed a seed about this ministry in my heart. My heart is not thorny and because it is not thorny, the **_Cares_** of this world cannot choke this word *(seed, Christ Our Life Ministries)* until it becomes unfruitful. Now, if you were to look at Christian broadcast stations all over the world, you would see that not all pastors live in this manner. Some have allowed *the deceitfulness of riches, to choke the word, until they become unfruitful.* Nevertheless, this ___Care___ exhibit is no different than Peter's in ___John 21:23___. Instead of them perfecting the saints for the work of the ministry, they have allowed themselves to be overtaken by thorns, the ___Care-s___ of this world and number one, the deceitfulness of riches. Note, they give the appearance that they ___Care___ for God's will being done in the earth but if you were to look at the anointing on their life and in their messages, it speaks against them. God could ___Care___ less if you prospered down here in this world as far as material things are concerned especially if you are not going to bless anybody through those blessings. God's desire is for church leaders, including myself, to teach believers entrusted to our ___Care___ His Word until these believers come unto the knowledge of the Son of God, unto a perfect man (*not a rich man as stated in ___Luke 18:25___*), unto the measure of the fulness of Christ because if we do not allow the Holy Spirit in us to teach them in this manner they will never overcome the lust of their earth suit.

In many of our services today, the ___Care___ for finances overshadows the Word of God. ___Malachi 3:5___ tells us that this oppression does not come from the Father. Please do not misunderstand me; I am not addressing every church; those leaders I am making reference to know who they are and ___Prov 27:20___ warns believers about these desires and the ___fact___ that they will never be satisfied no matter how much they oppress their members.

Pastors, you do not need a bigger church. Pastors, stop those long tithes and offering services that shouldn't last more than 5 to 10 minutes because you are determined to oppress your members until they give, give, and give when actually it is we who should do some giving to them. But most importantly, stop cursing the members of the *Body of Christ* who have nothing to give due to your ministries persistent request for finances so that you may consume it upon your fleshly lust *(James 4:3)*. Furthermore, *Malachi 3:8* does not apply to a child of God.

Some of you need to read that chapter starting at verse one and ask God to forgive you. *A child of God cannot be cursed for not obeying the teachings of the Law if they are walking and living in obedience to the Spirit.* Either teach them about tithes and offering through the eyes of Christ and in accordance with *2Tim 3:16* or do not teach it at all. Now, if you have been teaching them in accordance with *2Tim 3:16*, they now are accountable to *Heb 10:26* and God. You and I as church leaders are not judges *(Matt 7:1)* of what is or is not acceptable by God. I have encountered scores of people who believe, *not feel*, that *the church of today* does not have a *burden* to see its members prosper above the prosperity of the church. So pastors and laymen, who are guilty of this, please examine yourself (2Cor 13:5) and your ministry to see if *Ye* be in the faith then ask God to create within you a clean heart and renew a right spirit within you *(Psalms 51:10)* so that you may be a good Shepherd of God's Children *(John 21:15-17)*. Let's read *3John 1-4*, it reads,

"The elder unto the well-beloved Gaius, whom I love in the truth. Beloved, I wish above all things that thou mayest prosper and be in health, even as thy soul prospereth. For I rejoiced greatly, when the brethren came and testified of the truth that is in thee, even as thou walkest in the truth. I have no greater joy than to hear that my children walk in truth."

John is talking to Gaius, whom as *1Cor 1:14* tells us Paul had baptized, and in the *truth* with him *(John 17:17)*. John's wish *(Care)*; notice, *he wished it not prayed it*, was that *above all things Gaius mayest prosper and be in health*. Don't pray for someone to get rich in this world. *Mark 12: 41-44* is the perfect example of how we tend to lose sight of the one who gives the believer their riches. John is not stupid. He was very smart to make this wish for Gaius. Can you hear John praying for the LORD to make someone rich after observing how the craving for worldly riches destroyed Judas, Achin, Ananias, and Sapphira *(Acts 5:1-10)*? What do you think John meant when he said the words "*mayest prosper*?"

The word "prosper" in many churches today means, "*to be rich in this world*". I sure hope not, especially if they have read <u>*Eph 4:13*</u> because <u>*Eph 4:13*</u> gives us the meaning of prosperity that I am sure John is referring to. Furthermore, the dictionary defines prosper as, "*to succeed, to thrive*." Succeed in what? In the words written in <u>*Eph 4:13*</u>. Not in this world, especially when <u>*1John 2:15-17*</u> tells us not to love the world. Notice how I underlined the word, **_and_** in this Bible verse. Why? Because **_and_** is a conjunction word, it only added John's desires for Gaius together in the same sentence. John also wanted Gaius to be in good health. Why? Because Gaius was in the truth. Believers should always want their brothers and sisters living in the truth to be in good health. This way, you will not have to **_Care_** (*a troubling of a personality's mind that causes it to worry*) about them in this wicked world we sojourn in.

Let's look at Job, a man who feared God and eschewed evil. Eschewing evil means you do not **_Care_** about anything the devil tempts you with because your one desire is to please the Father. Job, Chapter 1, verses 1-5 says,

"*There was a man in the **land of Uz, whose name was Job**; and that man was perfect and upright, and one that feared God, and eschewed evil. **And there were born unto him seven sons and three daughters.** His substance also was seven thousand sheep, and three thousand camels, and five hundred yoke of oxen, and five hundred she asses, and a very great household; so that this man was the greatest of all the men of the east. **And his sons went and feasted in their houses, every one his day; and sent and called for their three sisters to eat and to drink with them. And it was so, when the days of their feasting were gone about, that <u>Job sent and sanctified them, and rose up early in the morning, and offered burnt offerings according to the number of them all: for Job said, It may be that my sons have sinned, and cursed God in their hearts. Thus did Job continually.</u>***"

Now, <u>*Job was not an Israelite, he was from the land of Uz, nor was he under the law Moses delivered unto the children*</u>

of Israel. He had something far greater; he had an intimate relationship with God. A relationship where he worshiped God in Spirit and in Truth *(John 4:24)*. But, even though he *feared God, and eschewed evil*, he did **_Care_** about his children. We know this because Job continually offered a burnt offering unto God according to the number of his children. Job knew that his children probably did not **_Care_** about worshipping God. Do you have children like this? Pastors, do you have members like this? If you do, does your lifestyle mirror the lifestyle resembling that of Job's? Is it like Job's when it comes to the **_Care_** you have for those you are accountable for? If so, then look at what happened after Satan answered the *LORD* and asked the *LORD* to test Job's true love for Him by removing the hedge of protection placed about *him, and about his house, and about all that he hath on every side*. Verses 9-13 and 18-22 read,

"*Then Satan answered the LORD, and said, Doth Job fear God for nought? Hast not thou made an hedge about him, and about his house, and about all that he hath on every side? thou hast blessed the work of his hands, and his substance is increased in the land. But put forth thine hand now, and touch all that he hath, and he will curse thee to thy face. And the LORD said unto Satan, Behold, all that he hath is in thy power; only upon himself put not forth thine hand. So Satan went forth from the presence of the LORD. And there was a day when his sons and his daughters were eating and drinking wine in their eldest brother's house.*

Verse 18-22, *While he was yet speaking, there came also another, and said, Thy sons and thy daughters were eating and drinking wine in their eldest brother's house: And, behold, there came a great wind from the wilderness, and smote the four corners of the house, and it fell upon the young men, and they are dead; and I only am escaped alone to tell thee. Then Job arose, and rent his mantle, and shaved his head, and fell down upon the ground, and worshipped, And said, Naked came I out of my mother's womb, and naked shall I return thither: the LORD gave, and the LORD hath taken away; blessed be the name of the LORD. In all this Job sinned not, nor charged God foolishly.*

If the *LORD* permitted Satan to do this to your children or church members, would you fall down and worship Him? Would you **Sin** not? Would you charge God foolishly? Because when our children or our church members do those things that we as parents and Pastors have preached over and over again *(Prov 29:1)*, and they fail to heed the instructions, our **Care** for them will be put to the test because the Word of God is truth *(John 17:17)*. It does not matter how much praying you have done for them, when the **Time** comes that *Satan has been given permission by God* to touch the things you **Care** about, he's going to make sure he touches them real good. Why? Because Satan knows he will not get very many opportunities to do that *(Psalms 91)*. Do you now see what Jesus was talking about in *John 16:33* when he said,

"*These things I have spoken unto you, that in me ye might have peace. In the world ye shall have tribulation: but be of good cheer; I have overcome the world.*"

You and I will have tribulations in this world. Satan will make sure of that in order to make you worry/**Care**. Therefore, make sure you inform your children and church members that you are praying for them but no matter how much **Time** you spend in prayer, *the Will of God is the Will of God*. Lot, Abraham's nephew had a wife who faced this test. In *Genesis 19:17-26*, we read,

"*And it came to pass, when they had brought them forth abroad, that he said, **Escape for thy life; look not behind** thee, neither stay thou in all the plain; escape to the mountain, lest thou be consumed. And Lot said unto them, Oh, not so, my Lord: Behold now, thy servant hath found grace in thy sight, and thou hast magnified thy mercy, which thou hast shewed unto me in saving my life; and I cannot escape to the mountain, lest some evil take me, and I die: Behold now, this city is near to flee unto, and it is a little one: Oh, let me escape thither, (is it not a little one?) and my soul shall live. And he said unto him, See, I have accepted thee concerning this thing also, that I will not overthrow this city, for the which thou hast spoken. Haste thee,* *escape thither; for I cannot do any thing till thou become thither. Therefore the name of the city was called Zoar. The sun was risen upon the earth when Lot entered into Zoar. Then the LORD rained upon Sodom and upon Gomorrah brimstone and fire from the LORD out of heaven; And he overthrew those cities, and all the plain, and all the inhabitants of the cities, and that which grew upon the ground. **But his wife looked back from behind him, and she became a pillar of salt.**"*

The *LORD* **Care**d enough about Lot and his family to save them from the *overthrew of those cities, and all the plain, and all the inhabitants of the cities, and that which grew upon the ground* and in like manner He **Care**d enough about us to send His only begotten Son to save His people *(believers)* from our Sins *(Matt 1:21)*. However, Mrs. Lot **Care**d more about what was in Sodom and Gomorrah than God's **Care** for her. In the world today, many of us exhibit this same lifestyle before God that Mrs. Lot exhibited. **Caring** more for this world than the salvation of their soul *(Romans 13:11)*. *We have got to stop **Care**-ing for the things of this world. They are hindering us from advancing forward in the things of God*. Let's look at *Luke 17: 31-37* which says,

*In that day, he which shall be upon the housetop, and his stuff in the house, <u>let him not come down to take it away</u>: and he that is in the field,<u> let him likewise not return back</u>. Remember Lot's wife. Whosoever shall seek to save his life shall lose it; and whosoever shall lose his life shall preserve it. I tell you, in that night there shall be **two men** in one bed; the one shall be taken, and the other shall be left. **Two women** shall be grinding together; the one shall be taken, and the other left. **Two men** shall be in the field; the one shall be taken, and the other left. And they answered and said unto him, Where, Lord? And he said unto them, Wheresoever the body is, thither will the eagles be gathered together.*

Do not come down from that housetop; do not return to that field. Let that worldly life you once **Care**d about when you walked according to the lust of your *Flesh* die *(John 12:24-25)*.

Also, *1Peter 2:19* foretells that you are going to encounter people who will mistreat you because you have chosen to let Christ be your life *(Col 3:4)*. But remember, **these are only tests.** Tests administered by God himself. Why? Because according to *Jer 17:10* God knows the wickedness of your heart but you don't. Your heart is the device that informs God, Satan, and everyone you come into contact with just who and what it is that you **_Care_** most about. That incident with my niece was a test of my heart to show me the **_Care_** I have for my family versus the **_Care_** I have for the things of God. You and I need to get a good picture of this parable Jesus is speaking here in *Luke 17*. The **two men**, the **two women**, and the other **two men**; One of them **_Care_**d more for themselves than God. The day of the LORD is the day that will declare it and when that day arrives, whomsoever found not living in obedience to it will not experience the joy of the rapture spoken about in *1Thes 4:16-18*. So, please read *1ˢᵗ Peter, Chapter 4* in its entirety.

I try not to **_Care_** if this book sells one copy. I have more important things to worry about than the selling of this book. I have a ministry to oversee. This book is a means of me being able to minister a message to the world wide Body of Christ that I otherwise would not be able to deliver in person. I have chosen to do what *Habakkuk 2:1-4* instructed me to do and live my life as though I haven't written a book. I chose to live and walk in *1 Peter 5:8-11*, which reads,

"Casting all your care upon him; for he careth for you. Be sober, be vigilant; because your adversary the devil, as a roaring lion, walketh about, seeking whom he may devour: Whom resist steadfast in the faith, knowing that the same afflictions are accomplished in your brethren that are in the world. But the God of all grace, who hath called us unto his eternal glory by Christ Jesus, after that ye have suffered a while, make you perfect, stablish, strengthen, settle you. To him be glory and dominion for ever and ever. Amen."

From the **Time** I send this book to the publisher until the breath of life departs my earth suit, I am not going to worry about something I have cast upon the Lord. So, I refuse to let the devil cause me to worry about the prosperity of this book because I have no power to make it increase. However, I know God and I know God can make it increase *(1Cor 3:6)*.

Flesh and Sin

*"O wretched man that I am! Who shall deliver me from
the body of this death?*
Romans 7:24

In this chapter, I shall be bold in my writing because I
truly believe that over ninety percent *(and I struggled to say
that)* of today's born-again believers do not have the slightest
idea of how wretched they are because of their earth suit *(Flesh)*
and its unification with **Sin** *(1John 1:8)*. Now, the thing that
prompts me to make such a bold statement as this is the lifestyle
they exhibit before the world and the unwise *(James 1:5)* choices
they are making every day that leads to **Death** *(Proverbs 16:25)*.
Unwise decisions that have them looking everywhere except
unto Jesus, the author and finisher of their faith *(Hebrews 12:2)*.
Now, I will stand in defense of some believers because the
individuals mostly at fault are the church leaders to whom these
believers have chosen as their spiritual leaders. Leaders who
consistently deliver unto them weekly messages that sound
nothing like the messages Christ and His Disciples taught to the
believers who believed in them *(Gal 1:8)*. Messages that
ministered life changing words to the hearer and caused a
transformation of the mind and filled the hearer with God-
consciousness; messages that quickened the hearer in their inner
man until they gladly received the Word, were baptized *(Acts
2:40-47)*, and accept Christ as their life *(Col 3:4)*.

In the world today, most of the messages I hear being
preached by some of these church leaders are messages that
address the first Adam image man, *the man living prior to the
Cross of Christ*; messages from the law that strengthen **Sin**
(1Cor 15:56). And the thing that saddens me the most is when
their members are overcome by the **Sin** in their **Flesh**, these
leaders and those loyal to them characterize these members as
backsliders while at the same **Time** living in ignorance of the
fact that perhaps if they would refrain from some of that singing
and hollering that they call church and begin to minister

messages unto them that cause conviction and *godly sorrow that worketh repentance to salvation not to be repented of (2Cor 7:10)*, that their members might have a change of heart and begin to live according to God's Word.

In this chapter, I will expound on verses 1-6. In these verses, the Apostle Paul speaks to the Roman Church and to the *teachers of the law* about the law and the power a law has over a man as long as he liveth and he paints a picture for us using the covenant of marriage to enlighten our minds so that we may see the **Dilemma** humans are faced with because of our soul and the breath of life in our nostrils being shut up within a Body of Sin **(Flesh)** as a result of the disobedience of the first man Adam. Therefore, to those of you who **profess to know the law**, what I write should not surprise you, **since you profess to know the law**.

Verse 1 says, *"Know ye not, brethren, (for I speak to them that know the law,) how that the law hath dominion over a man as long as he liveth."*

There are two key things Paul mentions in this verse that I will talk about and they are, *"them that know the law"* and *"dominion"*. What I shall write, I write boldly. In the short Time I have been in the ministry, I have encountered numerous Pastors' who claim to know the law but in **fact** do not know it. Now, I will say that they know what the law says. However, **knowing the law and knowing what the law SAYS are two completely different things**. Unless you have an intimate relationship with something or someone you will never know that person or thing but you will know what he/she/it says. Many people who say they believe God do not believe God; they only believe your belief about Him. Many people in the body of Christ know what the Bible says about Christ *(Light/written word)* but they do not know Christ as their life *(Phil 1:21)*. For if they did, they would *stop trying to live according to* the Law and *live according to* the law of the Spirit of life in Christ Jesus.

The LORD God kept no secrets from the first man Adam. The first man Adam was very much aware of both laws in *Genesis 2:16-17*. I can hear the LORD God saying this to the first man Adam concerning the forbidden tree, "*You eat, you die; You don't eat, you live*". He gave him instructions *(1Tim 3:16)* about the *law of life* when he <u>commanded him</u> saying, "*Thou shalt not eat of it*" and instructions about the *law of Death* when he <u>commanded him</u> saying "*for in the day that thou eatest thereof, thou shalt surely die (Soul, Ezek 18:4 and earth suit Gen 3:19)*. Please notice, In the beginning, the LORD God did not put the first man Adam under any law. The first man Adam, who was created in the image of God, was given freedom of choice as to which law he would subject himself and all men to. As we have discovered, we now know that he chose the *law of Death*. On the other hand, the last Adam *(Christ,1Cor 15:45-47)*, our Lord, chose to live by the law of the Spirit of life.

Now, concerning the law that Moses gave to the children of Israel could not give mankind the Christ-life *(Gal 3:21)*, the life men need to live eternally with God, nor could it stop the sting of *Death (1Cor 15:55)*. So, let's read verse one again.

Verse 1 says, "*Know ye not brethren, (for I speak to them that know the law), how that the law hath dominion over a man as long as he liveth?*"

Note again what Paul says. He says, "*the law hath dominion over a man as long as he liveth*". When the first man Adam and Eve ate from the forbidden tree, **they died to** *the law of the Spirit of life in Christ Jesus*. Their disobedience to the command of the LORD God sold them under **_Sin_**, giving the law of **_Sin_** dominion over their earthen vessel **_(Flesh)_**. The spiritual life they once knew did not die, their Earth Suit came to life as servants to **_Sin (Romans 6:6)_**. *The law of the Spirit of life in Christ*, they previously possessed, *is spiritual, it cannot die, and it applies only to the living*. What would it profit God to receive an offering from something dead *(Rom 6:12 & Rom 8:6)* seeing that He is the God of the living *(Matt 22:32)*? When the first man Adam and Eve became carnally minded, the grace of God kept them alive but they were now the servants of *Sin,* a law that reigns over all men until the day of **Death** if God does not make a way of escape for men. Now, until God made that way, men served the law of *Sin* with a carnal mind and according to *Romans 8:6*, *"To be carnally minded is Death"*. As long as a man or woman lives carnally minded, *the law of Sin and Death hath dominion over him/her as long as he/she liveth.* This law oppresses the soul to lust for the things of this world until the earth suit dies and then **Death** holds that soul if it has not believed in the Word of God, received baptism in Jesus name, and obey His *sayings and teachings (Mark 16:16).* If the soul does not die to *Sin,* it will never gain our it's liberty from **Death**'s power and when the Lord raises us from the dead, that soul will be raised under Death's power and judged out of those things written in the books, according to their works as mentioned in *Revelation 20:12-13.*

Now, Verses 2 through 4 took me some **Time** to get revelation knowledge on. These three verses define Romans Chapter 7. If you do not pay attention to the sudden change made between verses 3 and 4, you will never be able to grasp the true meaning of how men are delivered from the law. I had to listen to these three verses on my MP3 player *repeatedly* before I finally got a break through *(Matt 5:6).*

Verse 2 says, *"For the woman which hath an husband is bound by the law to her husband so long as he liveth; but if the husband be dead, she is loosed from the law of her husband."*

*"For the woman which hath an husband (**the body of Sin**) is bound by the law (**Sin**) to her husband so long as he liveth; but if the husband (**the body of Sin**) be dead, she is loosed from the law (**Sin**) of her husband."*

I know this might sound strange asking this question following that paragraph but do you know what the purpose of water baptism is? What it is symbolical of? Church leaders should know. Water baptism symbolizes the taking off and burial *(Death)* of the image of the first man Adam *(Gen 5:3)* and his sinful ways. Let's read *Hebrews 2:14* and get a better understanding of what I am saying. It reads,

Forasmuch then as the children are partakers of flesh and blood, <u>he also himself likewise took part of the same; that through death he might destroy him that had the power of death</u>, that is, the devil.

Water Baptism, is a principle established by God as a prelude leading to any life changing event in the Bible that deals with spiritual matters. He applied it to Noah and the flood, Moses and the Children of Israel as they departed Egypt through the Red Sea, Joshua and the Children of Israel as they crossed over the River Jordan into the promised land, Elijah and Elisha walking through the River Jordan before Elijah was raptured away in a fiery chariot out of Heaven *(2Kings 2:11-15)*, and John the Baptist for the preparation of Souls as he readied them for the arrival of the Messiah *(Mal 3:1, John 1:22-27)*.   However, none of these baptisms could save a man from their ***Sins***, only water baptism in Jesus name can do that. Why? Because Jesus is the Word made ***Flesh*** *(John 1:14)* and the person God sent to save his people from their ***Sins***. How? *Titus 3:4-6* and *Hebrews 2:14*.

When the first man Adam's transgression made all men *partakers of flesh and blood, He **(Jesus, the last Adam)** also himself likewise took part of the same; that through **Death** He might destroy him that had the power of death, that is, the devil.* Furthermore, the Word of God, according to *Philippians 2:7-8*, says that He *made himself of no reputation, and took upon him the form of a servant, and was made in the likeness of men: And being found in fashion as a man, he humbled himself, and became obedient unto death, even the death of the cross* and now, according to *Galatians 3:27*, whosoever that has been baptized into Christ have put on Christ and according to *Galatians 3:10*, when you put on Christ, which is done through believing and water baptism, *you have put on the new man, which is renewed in knowledge after the image of him that created him.*

However, there are church leaders who continue to believe that born again believers, people who have been baptized in Jesus name and become what *2 Cor 5:17* says they are, should subject themselves, after having *put on the new man* to the laws and ordinances *(Col 2:20)* handed down by Moses. Now, *2 Cor 5:17* says,

"Therefore if any man be in Christ, he is a new creature: old things are passed away; behold, all things are become new."

If any man (*soul*) be in Christ, he is a new creature *(Child of God)*, old things are passed away *(the first man Adam image)*; behold, all things are become new *(the Christ life)"*. Believers now possess a new life, a life that according to *2Cor 5:21*, knew no **Sin**. So, let's see what Paul in **verse 2** teaches us *(Romans 10:17)*.

If a woman *(Soul)* which hath a husband *(the body of **Sin**)* is bound by the law *(**Sin**)* to her husband *(the body of **Sin**)* so long as he *(the body of **Sin**)* liveth. But if the husband *(the body of **Sin**)* be dead, she *(Soul)* is loosed from the law *(Sin)* of her husband *(the body of **Sin**)*. Therefore, she *(Soul)* is free to remarry whoever she *(Soul)* wants *(Christ 2Cor 11:2)*.

*The law of **Sin** and **Death** because of the first man Adam's disobedience is now in a covenant relationship with our **Flesh** and for this reason, the LORD God cursed all **Flesh** to die *(Gen 3:19)* and appointed a day that it shall die *(Gen 2:17 & Heb 9:27)*. He did not curse the soul, but if the soul **Sins**, it will die *(Ezek 18:4)* along with the **Flesh** in the lake of fire.

Now, please hear this. The liberty that we as born again believers received in Christ which delivered us from the law of **Sin** does not give you the licensure to go and get a divorce just because you and your spouse disagree to a point that those disagreements harden your hearts toward each other and you start hearing a small voice speak a word into your **ears** called *"divorce" (Mark 4:23)*. You must always be aware of the *law of* **Sin**. This law cannot die and it is going to entice you to serve it

61

and obey the lust of your **_Flesh_**. Now, if this **_Sin_** gets to where it is to overbearing, you must look unto Jesus, the author and finisher of your faith *(Heb 12:2)* because apart from Him *(John 15:5)* you will not defeat Satan, the devil, the god of this world, and his oppressive counselings *(Psalms 1:1)* aimed at blinding you to the truths of God's Word *(2Cor 4:3-4)* and what it has to say about *"divorce" (Mark 10:2-12)*. Furthermore, Christians must remember another thing. When we stop looking unto Jesus to solve the problems we experience in life or in our marriages, *the law of **Sin*** dwelling in our supposedly crucified **_Flesh_**, will become revived *(Rom 7:9)* and oppress us to a point that we start living that first man Adam imaged lifestyle we lived prior to water baptism and spiritual rebirth *(John 3:5)* in Jesus name.

Now to those of you who got a divorce and your husband is still alive on this earth and you have not *put on the new man, Christ, which is renewed in knowledge after the image of him that created him*, then *according to the vows of your marriage*, you cannot remarry unless your marriage partner dies (*the law of marriage hath dominion over a man as long as he liveth, as I mentioned earlier, a law cannot die*). Therefore, if you remarry and your mate is not dead, then according to *the Law of God* that Moses gave to the Children of Israel, you are an adulteress, a **_Sinner_**. I do not **_Care_** what anyone says, **_you made a vow_** and *Prov 6:2/Ecc 5:4-6* give instructions that warn about the breaking of a vow. However, rebirth of the Spirit and the *law of the Spirit of life in Christ Jesus* addresses the **_Sinners_** of this world who now believe in *(John 3:17)* and have made Him their High Priest, by a new commandment *(Hebrews 7:12-19)* . Let's read *John 8:3-11*. It reads,

*"And the scribes and Pharisees brought unto him a woman taken in adultery; and when they had set her in the midst, They say unto him, Master, this woman was taken in adultery, in the very act. Now **Moses in the law commanded** us, that such should be stoned: but what sayest thou? This they said, tempting him, that they might have to accuse him. But Jesus stooped down, and with his finger wrote on the ground, as though he heard them not. So when they continued asking him, he lifted up*

*himself, and said unto them, He that is without **Sin** among you, let him first cast a stone at her. And again he stooped down, and wrote on the ground. And they which heard it, being convicted by their own conscience, went out one by one, beginning at the eldest, even unto the last: and Jesus was left alone, and the woman standing in the midst. When Jesus had lifted up himself, and saw none but the woman, he said unto her, Woman, where are those thine accusers? hath no man condemned thee? She said, No man, Lord. And Jesus said unto her, **Neither do I condemn thee: go, and sin no more**.*

This lady who had committed adultery in the eyes of a *law of the Spirit of life in Christ Jesus* child **did commit a trespass but is not condemned** *(Rom 8:1)*, she receives grace *(Rom 5:20)*. However, this lady in the eyes of the *law of God given by Moses* teacher, condemns and makes that trespass look exceedingly **Sin**-fuller than the trespasses they themselves commit on a daily basis. However, Christ, *(the last Adam)* had something to say to these *that know the law* scribes and Pharisees. He said, "*He that is without **Sin** among you, let him first cast a stone at her*."

Upon hearing this, they left convicted of **their own conscience**. Why? They knew they were **Sinners** too. Does your conscience convict you when you judge people because of what the law saith *(Rom 3:19)* instead of grace? It should. *1John 1:8* tells us all that we are not without **Sin**. So, would you church leaders who **profess to know the law** please observe how Jesus handled this lady who was caught in adultery? He said, "*Woman, where are those thine accusers*".

Now I wonder, if I were to ask to a born again believer who attends your church services and was caught in adultery or has been divorced if they would tell me that they know of individuals in *the body of Christ* who persistently condemn them for getting divorced, then remarried, or for committing adultery in regards to something they did when they walked according to the course of this world fulfilling the dictates of their **Flesh** during the **Time** they obeyed the lust of it prior to coming to

Christ. Some of you know who I am talking to. Yeah, I am talking to you. You so called Word of God experts reading this book. Either teach *the law of the Spirit of life in Christ Jesus* or teach *the Law of Moses*. However, If the person you are addressing is a new creature in Christ, leave them alone if they have been walking in obedience to the Word of God since being converted from the error of their previous ways *(James 5:20)*. Look at Jesus' closing statement to this woman, "*Jesus said unto her, Neither do I condemn thee: go, and **Sin** no more*". Not go and get out of that marriage or you can't remarry. Christ taught this lady the meaning of *John 3:17*, a verse that says,

> "*For God sent not his Son into the world to **condemn** the world; but that the world through him might be saved.*"

The problem in *the Body of Christ* today is that born again believers are not allowing other born again believers walking in obedience to God's Word to enjoy the liberty they received after accepting Christ *(Gal 2:4)* and being raised from the dead *(Eph 2:1-7, water baptism)*. Now, if the person hasn't been born again, you are correct in your teaching. However, if they have been born-again, and are obeying the *teachings and sayings of Christ*, then they live by a new law *(Romans8:2,James2:12)*, under a new dispensation, a dispensation known as **the dispensation of grace** *(Eph 1:10 & 3:2)*. I **speak this to them who know the law, since you profess to know the law.**

It amazes me that God, who takes the foolish things of this world to confound the wise, has *not to any fault of His own*, confounded those who say they **know the law** and **His Word**. Some of our church leaders are confounded by the Gospel message but they'll tell you God called them into the ministry. **Yeah, they said it** *(Prov 6:2)*. We who call ourselves teachers better know what we are talking about *(James 3:1)* especially when it comes to addressing *the Body of Christ (Matthew 18:6-7)*. We are preachers of the Gospel and our message is to be preached so that mankind may come to know the love God has for them and that He wants to save them and give them eternal life, not a condemning life.

In *Genesis, Chapter 3*, the LORD God initiated no way for the first man Adam to regain a spirit filled eternal life with Him after he and Eve ate from the Tree of the Knowledge of Good and Evil nor did the giving of His Law to Moses make a way for the Children of Israel to receive everlasting life either. The Law of Moses was God's demand on the ***Flesh***; God's demand on all who bear the image of the first man Adam to show men how wretched they are *(Rom 7:24 / Rev 3:17)* and their need of a Savior.

Without Christ, man has no way of returning to God and It was not until *"God sent forth his Son, made of a woman, made under the law (Mosaic), to redeem them that were under the law (Gal 4:4-5)"* that the Israelites had a way of giving God the true Worship He has always desired of men *(John 4:24)*. A way paved by His grace and mercy. We serve a gracious God *(Eph 2:8)*. The law is not gracious. When the first man Adam ***committed spiritual adultery***, you will not find it written anywhere in the Bible where the LORD God tried to stone him to ***Death***? No, the LORD God showed him grace and mercy *(Romans 9:15)*. The law is not so, it demands ***Death***, and believe me, every day men violate the law, including myself at ***Times***. I just want to be real before you. God knows Minister Redd. What will it profit me to lie to you? You cannot save me.

Verse 3 says, *"So then if, while her husband liveth, she be married to another man, she shall be called an adulteress: but if her husband be dead, she is free from that law; so that she is no adulteress, though she be married to another man."*

*So then if, while her husband (the body of **Sin**) liveth and she(Soul)be married to another man (the body of **Sin**), she(Soul) shall be called an adulteress (**law given by Moses**): but if her husband (the body of **Sin**) be dead, she(Soul) is free from that law (**law given by Moses**); so that she(Soul) is no adulteress, though she(Soul) be married to another man (Christ Jesus).*

Prior to a man/woman accepting Christ as their life and being baptized, that man/woman bears the image of the first Adam, the father of all **_Flesh_**, and a servant of **_Sin_**, as stated in _Romans 6:20_. When that man or woman accepts Christ as their life, _Notice, accepts Christ as their life, and dies to the first Adam image life_, but continues to live the first Adam image life of the **_Flesh_**, this person _shall be called an adulteress._ However, if that person _"through the Spirit mortifies the deeds of the **Flesh**"_, that person is _free from that law; so that he/she is no adulteress, though he/she be married to another woman/man._ Now remember, if you have not mortified your earth suit, the law says you are an adulteress, not Minister Redd. I told you before that the law cannot die nor will God remove it until heaven and earth pass away. Look at what Jesus says in _Matthew 5:18_,

"For verily I say unto you, **Till heaven and earth pass**, one jot or one tittle **shall in no wise pass from the law**, till all be fulfilled".

You will have to fulfill every vow you made in your **_Flesh_** if you do not mortify it. _**All laws are spiritual and they remain the same all the time, allowing no exceptions**_. Gravity is a law and it will never stop pulling things back to the earth. The _law of **Sin** and **Death**_ is no different. It will not stop trying to pull a believer back into that old carnal lifestyle they received from the first man Adam _(Luke 11:24-26 & James 1:2-4, the **Care**-ing life)_ at birth.

Paul was the first person in the Bible to explain **_Sin_** as being a law. This was a very important discovery and has opened my eyes to where I can better understand the scriptures and brings into perspective the **_Dilemma_** all men are faced with. However, as sad as it is to say, we have church leaders who have been Christians for many years yet have not come to see **_Sin_** as a law but teach people about the law. Somebody didn't like that. Nevertheless, you better stay open minded to this teaching and receive this light that I am communicating to you. Let's read

John 4:16-18, and examine a conversation Jesus had with a woman of Samaria.

"***Jesus saith*** *unto her, Go,* ***call thy husband,*** *and come hither.* ***The woman*** *answered and* ***said, I have no husband.*** ***Jesus said*** *unto her,* ***Thou hast well said, I have no husband:*** ***For thou hast had five husbands; and he whom thou now hast*** ***is not thy husband:*** *in that saidst thou truly.*"

What we just read in reality, was a conversation between Jesus and a servant of *Sin*. A conversation between Jesus and a soul living in Samaria. However, nowhere in their conversation did we hear about the *Death* of either of her husbands. Most importantly, nowhere in the conversation did Jesus condemn this lady either. *Her own conscience condemned her (Rom 2:14)*. **Jesus addressed *her* ignorance**, ("*The woman answered and said, I have no husband)*" **with the truth,** ("*Thou hast well said, I have no husband: For thou hast had five husbands; and he whom thou now hast is not thy husband: in that saidst thou truly*)". The dictionary defines *ignorance* as, "*lack of knowledge, education, or awareness.*"

Was Jesus' reply to her unsympathetic? Let's read verse 19 and find out.

"*The woman saith unto him, Sir, I perceive that thou art a prophet.*"

No, it was not unsympathetic. His reply did not make her angry, nor did she get up and leave. She acknowledged Jesus as a prophet. Why? He told her the truth. *The truth about herself.* Not about what she did wrong or that she was in an adulterous relationship with another man. This is true Christianity. Jesus' reply and her submission to His *words of truth* caused the conversation about her husbands to become a dead subject; turning it into a spiritual life changing one. If men and women would just receive the truth, arguments and disagreements would never manifest and people could meet daily in the temple, and in every house, ceasing not to teach and preach Jesus Christ" *(Acts*

5:42). Which is exactly what the second part of Romans 7, verse 3 is talking about? Life in Christ, the last Adam. "*But if her husband be dead (the first man Adam image), she is free from that law (law given by Moses); so that she is no adulteress, though she be married to another man.*"

After a person accepts Christ as Lord and Savior of their life and is baptized, that person obtains a new life. The life of Christ, the life of the last Adam, the life that, *2Cor 5:21 & 1John 3:5* says knew no **Sin**. It is the life the first man Adam possessed and would have passed onto us had he not eaten from the forbidden tree. A person professing to be a Christian is a spiritual minded individual who has mortified the deeds of the Flesh, and are walking in the newness of that life *(Romans 6:4)*.

The men and women who obey the teaching of *Acts 2:36* are new creatures in Christ Jesus. They are people who have had their consciences purged from dead works, and have no idea what you are talking about when you speak to them concerning that prior lifestyle they once lived when they were the servants of **Sin** and obeyed the lust of their **Flesh**. However, they know who you are *(Rev 12: 10-11)*.

Verse 4 says, "*Wherefore, my brethren,* **Ye also are become dead to the law by the body of Christ**; *that ye should be married to another, even to him who is raised from the dead, that we should bring forth fruit unto God.*

Do you see the change? In verses 2 and 3, the husband *(the body of Sin)* must die in order for men not to be called an adulteress but in verse 4 it is actually the **Soul** that must die. What makes me say that? The word **Ye**. According to Genesis 2:7, **Ye**, became a living soul and Gen 2:14 says that, "*thou* **(Ye)** *shalt surely die*". When the first man Adam sinned, **Ye (soul)** became a Sinner. *The Law of* **Sin** *mingled with* **Ye's Flesh** in reality does not die, but **Ye** can reckon its **Flesh**, *the body of Sin* as dead *(Rom 6:11)*. It is through water baptism and rebirth of the Spirit that **Ye** makes this possible. Water baptism places **Ye**, the soul, in **the body of Christ**. Water baptism delivers **Ye** from the power of **Death**. All born of the water and of the Spirit believers *(Ye's)* are dead to the *law of **Sin*** and **Death** because of the body of Christ.

Who was *the body of Christ*? Jesus. Was Jesus? Jesus was the Word made **Flesh**? Yes, **Flesh.** *John 1:14* tells us that He was. Did Jesus die? Yes. Is Jesus Alive? Yes. Read *Acts 2:22-24, 31-32, and 36*. But today, we see people who profess Christ to be their life living the lifestyle the first man Adam imaged person lived thus proving that they have not "*reckoned **Ye** also yourselves to be dead indeed unto **Sin** (Rom 6:11)* which makes them adulteress to *the law of the Spirit of life in Christ Jesus,* and repeating over again what the first man Adam and Eve did in the beginning.

Verse 5 says, "*For when we were in the flesh, the motions of sins, which were by the law, did work in our members to bring forth fruit unto death.*

Let me start this verse off by laying a foundation. *If a man*, Jew or Gentile, *is not in Christ, he/she is in the first man Adam, a earthly man (1Cor 15:47)* and because he/she is in the first Adam*, the motions of **Sins**, which were by the law, did work in his/her members to bring forth fruit unto **Death***. Before water baptism and rebirth of the Spirit *(John 3:5)*, Men by nature are born carnal in the **Flesh** and the motions of **Sins**, which were by the *law*, worked in our **Flesh** to bring forth fruit unto **Death** and in *Galatians 5: 19-21*, we are told of these works. They are,

"*Now **the works of the flesh are manifest**, which are these; Adultery, fornication, uncleanness, lasciviousness, Idolatry, witchcraft, hatred, variance, emulations, wrath, strife, seditions, heresies, Envyings, murders, drunkenness, revellings, and such like: of the which I tell you before, as I have also told you in time past, that they which do such things shall not inherit the kingdom of God.*"

Why is adultery first? Because adultery actually stands for unfaithfulness. Unfaithfulness in a relationship is the foundation from whence all **Sins** arise. Remember, Eve was deceived, but the first man Adam *willfully* chose to be unfaithful. Therefore, since the first man Adam willfully *(Hebrews 10:26)* chose to be unfaithful, every male and female born of **Flesh** and blood bears his unfaithful life *(sinful Romans 8:3)*. A life that the first man Adam chose when he ate of the forbidden fruit. *If you eat forbidden fruit you are a partaker of forbidden fruit.* What does partake mean? Webster's says that *partake* means "*to possess or share a certain nature or attribute*". For this reason, men born in the image of the first man Adam also possess his nature *(Gen 4:1, 5:3)*. Meaning any man *not born again of water and of Spirit* can only bring God fruit unto **Death**. This is why Abraham could not sacrifice Isaac. Even though Isaac was a son of promise, he still bore the image of the first man Adam. How do we know this? He Died. Cain, the first man Adam's first child teaches us the best. Cain brought of the fruit of the ground an offering unto the Lord *(Gen 3:3)*. Cain was born in the first Adam's image. An image corrupted by **Sin's** evil nature *(2Peter 1:4/Romans 8:21)* and due to this nature being united with in every man's **Flesh**, **all Flesh** has corrupted its way upon the earth as mentioned in *Genesis 6:11-13*. How? Through *the motions of* **Sins**, *which were by the law; a law that is constantly at work in our members bringing us unto* **Death**. **Death** corrupts the **Flesh**, But **Sin** corrupts the Soul *(Ezek 18:4)*.

Verse 6 says, "*But now we are delivered from the law, that being dead wherein we were held; that we should serve in newness of spirit, and not in the oldness of the letter.*"

Romans Chapter 6 deals with man's deliverance from **Sin**. This chapter deals with man's deliverance from the law. Why church leaders in certain denominations who say they are part of the five-fold ministry described in *Eph 4:11* subject men and women in *the Body of Christ* to the teachings of the law is beyond me. Christ gave clear instructions in *Matt 9:17* that, "*Neither do men put new wine into old bottles: else the bottles break, and the wine runneth out, and the bottles perish: but they put new wine into new bottles, and both are preserved.*" Church leaders who teach their members *in the oldness of the letter* say they are showing them examples of how God dealt with the Nation of Israel are failing to realize that the hearers they are addressing bears the image of Christ and serve in the newness of the spirit, _not in the oldness of the letter_ (Moses Law Matt 17:1-5), **_hear ye him_**. Believers walking in obedience to God's Word do not need the law and _1Timothy1:9-10_ support this statement. These verses say,

"Knowing this, that **the law is not made for a righteous man,** but for the lawless and disobedient, for the ungodly and for sinners, for unholy and profane, for murderers of fathers and murderers of mothers, for manslayers, [10] For whoremongers, for them that defile themselves with mankind, for menstealers, for liars, for perjured persons, and if there be any other thing that is contrary to sound doctrine."

Believers are righteous men _(Rom 4:3)_. Men who the law is not made for. Righteous men need faith. Faith that comes by hearing and hearing by the Word of God _(Rom 10:17, John 1:14-Jesus)_ which is who Jesus was, _"But before faith came, we were kept under the law, shut up unto the faith which should afterwards be revealed. Wherefore the law was our schoolmaster to bring us unto Christ, that we might be justified by faith. But after that faith is come, we are no longer under a schoolmaster. For ye are all the children of God by faith in Christ Jesus. For as many of us as have been baptized into Christ have put on Christ."(Galatians 3:23-27)_

I'll end this Chapter with _Romans 6:3-14._ But again, I find it hard to believe that men and women who **_profess to know the law_** do not know the law. These verses says,

"Know ye not, that so many of us (Men and Women) as were baptized into Jesus Christ were baptized into his **Death**? Therefore we are buried with him by baptism into **Death**: that like as Christ was raised up from the dead by the glory of the Father, even so we also should walk in newness of life. For if we have been planted together in the likeness of his **Death**, we shall be also in the likeness of his resurrection: Knowing this, that our *old man is crucified with him, that **THE BODY OF SIN** might be destroyed, that henceforth we should not serve sin. For **he that is dead is freed from sin**. Now if we be dead with Christ, we believe that we shall also live with him: Knowing that Christ being raised from the dead dieth no more; **Death** hath no more dominion over him. For in that he died, he died unto **Sin** once: but in that he liveth, he liveth unto God. Likewise reckon **ye** also yourselves to be dead indeed unto **Sin**, but alive unto God through Jesus Christ our Lord. Let not **Sin** therefore reign in your mortal body, that ye should obey it in the lusts thereof. Neither yield ye your members as instruments of unrighteousness unto **Sin**: but yield yourselves unto God, as those that are alive from the dead, and your members as instruments of righteousness unto God. For **Sin shall not have dominion** over you: **for Ye are not under the law, but under grace**." **Sin** shall* not have dominion over you. *Sin* should not have dominion over you.

Death

*O wretched man that I am! who shall deliver me
from the body of this death?*
Romans 7:24

Death is all around us. The **_Death_** of family members, friends, neighbors, acquaintances, and animals. Yet, no one wants to talk about **_Death_** or why every creature on earth experiences it. I personally do not mind talking about **_Death_** and the reason why I do not mind is because everyone needs to know that as soon a person is born into this world, the earthen vessel they enter into this world with is said by scripture to be *the Body of Sin*. A body the LORD God cursed to die. A body laden with lustful thoughts; something that *James 1:15* says "*when lust hath conceived, it bringeth forth* **Sin:** *and* **Sin,** *when it is finished, bringeth forth* **_Death_**".

Death is a reality. Anything that is a reality should be talked about and not feared *(Heb 2:15, 2Tim 1:7)*. Everyday, the obituary section of our newspapers and the grave yards testify of its existence and dominion over the **Flesh**. Furthermore, *2Cor 5:10-11* declares that God has appointed a day when **_Death_** is going to bring us all before the judgment seat of Christ to be judged of the Lord for the things done in our earth suit whether they be good or bad. Oh, we'll talk about hurricanes, tornados, terrorist, and the damages caused by them. Yet, we refuse to talk about this well-known spirit associated with those disasters that men typically face on an everyday basis *(Revelation 6:8)*. Disasters that sometime bring unforgettable and unforgivable pain to the loved ones of those caught in their paths. Do you know what the name of this spirit is? It is the spirit of **_Death_** and the Bible speaks volumes about it. Why? Because **_Everything will pass through it gates_**. In **_fact_**, there are 491 verses in the Bible that mention **_Death_**. Not only does the Bible speak volumes about **_Death_,** *Heb 2:14* even addresses *the one who once had* the power of **_Death_**.

DEATH AND HELL

Now, *Genesis 37:34-35 & Job 2:13* are two verses of scripture addressing some of man's grief that **Death** causes. Furthermore, there is no weapon on earth capable of making men feel so much pain and grief in their heart than **Death**. Now, to most people, **Death** symbolizes the end of a person's life and something the Devil takes great delight in knowing that most men and women only hold a minute level of knowledge about. Why? Because he knows that **Death** encompasses much more than that. Satan's greatest fear is that men and women will one day finally *hear* and understand the *teachings and sayings of John 8:51 & Acts 2:24*. Teachings that bring conviction to the hearts of the hearers, not condemnation. Teachings that quicken men in their hearts to repent of their wicked ways *(2Chron 7:14)*. But most importantly, teachings about the spirit of **Death**; the spirit engulfing man's entire world and holding *everyone who does not keep the teachings and sayings of Jesus Christ* forever in its bondage *(Acts 2:24)*.

Now, what I wrote should not come as a surprise to some of you because the Word of God has been warning humanity about **Death** since the beginning of *Time*. The LORD God spoke about **Death** in the Garden of Eden to the first man Adam who at the *Time* lived in a world void of **Death**. Nevertheless, rather than live in the world God created for them, the first man Adam and Eve chose to live in a world ruled by **Death**. A world that has made men out to be slaves to **Sin** and receive wages unto **Death**. The first man Adam's transgression of the LORD God's command along with his wife to not eat of the Tree of the Knowledge of Good and Evil alienated themselves and all men from the life of God; now, all men are born in the first man Adam's image; an image that receives wages unto **Death**. Furthermore, according to *Exodus 32:7 & Gal 3:22* it does not matter if you are a Jew or Gentile, you are born in this image and because you are born this way, *Heb 9:27* tells us that we are appointed to die. Why? Because this is the only way men gain liberty from Sin's power. Now, to those of you who refuse to believe what I have written, the Word of God says in *Romans 5:12* that,

74

"*__Death__ passed upon all men, for that __all__ have sinned*"

And in *Acts 17:26* it says, "*And hath made of __one blood__ all nations of men for to dwell on all the face of the earth, and hath determined the __Times__ before appointed, and the bounds of their habitation*".

The first Adam passed *__Death__* upon all men through one blood and according to the teaching of *Heb 9:27,* God has *determined the __Times__* as to how long men shall be *bound of this habitation.* The first man Adam's transgression of the LORD God's commandment gave *__Sin__* a place of habitation. That place of habitation is our *__Flesh__*; our earth suit that scripture calls *the Body of Sin.* Also dwelling within this body is our soul and the breath of life. The only way to get them these two components that complete man is *__Death__*. If it were up to the devil, men would never die. The devil loves to have the preeminence over men. That is why he was cast out of heaven. He wanted to have the preeminence over heaven at first *(Isaiah 14:13)*. However, God did not create men to be Satan or *__Sin__*'s servants. He created men to "*Be fruitful, and multiply, and replenish the earth, and subdue it: and have dominion over the fish of the sea, and over the fowl of the air, and over every living thing that moveth upon the earth*" *(Gen 1:28)*, not the servants of a fallen angel. Nevertheless, the first man Adam's transgression in the beginning made all men servants of *__Sin__* *(Rom 6:17)* through his one blood *(Acts 17:26)*.

Now, we know that blood is probably the most valuable thing on the earth. But I want you to know that it can also be the most dangerous. Why? Let's read *Leviticus 17:14*, it says,

"*__For it is the life of all flesh__; the blood of it is for the life thereof: therefore I said unto the children of Israel, Ye shall eat the blood of no manner of flesh: __for the life of all flesh is the blood__ thereof: whosoever eateth it shall be cut off,* on this earth".

Blood is the life of the *__Flesh__*. Not air, but blood. When the first man Adam ate of the forbidden tree, his disobedience brought **Death** into the world and into the blood stream of every earthen vessel making our earth suits according to _Romans 7:24_, **bodies of Death**. Furthermore, _Romans 8:18-22_ tells us that everyone born of **Flesh** and blood, inherit this **one blood**. It is also a known **fact** that children inherit the blood of their parents. Therefore, if the parents' blood is corruptible, the child's blood likewise will also be corruptible _(Matthew 7:17)_. Living within this blood is a nature. A nature called **Sin** and this nature bringeth for **Death** to every living thing. This nature of **Sin is a law**. It cannot die. However, earthen vessels can. So, whatever the nature of a creature is, as long as its earth suit is good and healthy, its nature will abide until the end of **Time**.

In our world today, whenever there is the slightest sign of a specific nature's earthen vessel becoming extinct, humans go to all sorts of lengths to ensure that that specific nature's earth suit is preserved and protected so future generations may enjoy it. Nevertheless, if the humans who spend incalculable amounts of hours **Caring** for these nearly extinct creatures would read their Bibles, they'd discover that not only is **Death** one day going to sting these creatures' but mankind as well _(1Cor 15:55)_. Today, we have so many educated scholars like the ones mentioned in _Psalms 14:1-4 & Romans 1:18-32_, living a life void of God-consciousness but speak as though they know everything about the creatures God created and the history of these creatures. Furthermore, men who live in this manner are the one's lacking God-consciousness and due to this lack of knowledge which is clearly mentioned in _Hosea 4:6_, Satan, the enemy of God, and also the god of this world has been able to keep these peoples minds and the minds of other humans who accept their teachings blinded to the _sayings and teachings of Jesus Christ,_ lest the light of the glorious gospel of Christ, who is the image of God, should shine unto them _(2 Cor 4:3-4)_ and cause them to repent and accept Christ as their life. However, looking at the spiritual condition of the human populace today, anyone can vividly see that Satan's blinding power of the human mind is thick and very dark evidenced by the relationship men have with this world and other men despite the **fact** that the

Word of God has given men warnings about loving this world. In *1John 2:15-17*, the Word says,

"*Love not the world, neither the things that are in the world. If any man love the world, the love of the Father is not in him. For all that is in the world, the lust of the flesh, and the lust of the eyes, and the pride of life, is not of the Father, but is of the world. And the world passeth away, and the lust thereof: but he that doeth the will of God abideth for ever.*"

The Lord, His Disciples, and the Five-Fold Ministry *(Eph 4:11)* has been warning *(Prov 29:1)* men not to love this world since the beginning of *Time*. Why? First, because Satan is the god of this world and he is God's number enemy. Secondly, *Rev 21:1* informs us that this world and everything associated with it will one day pass away. *Time* is running out on this world but men are living as though it will not. Satan on the other hand, knows that *Man's Time* on earth is running out. Therefore, he stays diligent in the affairs of men keeping them in spiritual strongholds *(2Cor 10:4)* that hinder men from seeking after God or desiring a relationship with Him and His Son, Christ Jesus. Now, the first man Adam made it easy for Satan to achieve this goal when he sinned, became a sinner, and through one blood made all men sinners. Therefore, because we have the nature and blood of a sinner, we *Sin*. *Sin* is the door through which **_Death_** is able to enter our lives. **_Death_** does not *Care* how it enters a persons life. When *Sin* opens a door for it, it is coming and it respects no man *(Gen 4:7)*.

Now the Bible refers to **_Death_** as being carnally minded and According to *Romans 8:6*, "*to be carnally minded is **Death**; but to be spiritually minded is life and peace*". This means that anyone born of the will of the *Flesh* and of blood is a carnally minded individual and servants of *Sin (Rom 6:17-20)*. *Sin* is mingled with and works in our earth suit, bringing everything living associated with it to **_Death_**. So, unless a man or woman is born again of the water and of the Spirit and receive Christ as their life, they will die carnally minded and **_Death_** will be their holding cell if they die before Jesus returns to earth without repenting of their **Sins** as told by the writer of Job in *Job 14:12*. On the other hand, according to *Acts 2:24* the scriptures tell us that **Death** could not hold Jesus. Why? Because Jesus was not carnally minded; Jesus was the Word made **Flesh**, He was spiritually-minded. It was the Will of God that made Jesus **Flesh** but it was the disobedience of the first man Adam that made himself and us **Flesh**. **Sinful Flesh** that is. Jesus walked under the authority of God's Word, not under **Sin** *(Romans 7:14)*. The first man Adam refused to walk under the authority of God's Word, but under **Sin**. So, let me state again what **Death** is. **Death** is carnal mindedness. Carnal mindedness means that you are more conscious of yourself, this world and the things of this world than the Will of God being done in the earth or in your life. Anyone conscious of self dwelleth in carnal mindedness.

Believers and unbelievers alike are prone to living a life of this stature. Yes, believers too. Do you brush your teeth, comb your hair, try to look good and dress nice just to impress people? Do you always want things yet love to recite Psalms 23:1, "*The Lord is my shepherd; I shall not want*. Everybody wants something. even God. Let's read *Galatians 5:17*, it reads,

"*For the flesh lusteth against the Spirit, and the Spirit against the flesh: and these are contrary the one to the other: so that ye cannot do the things that ye would.*"

God lusteth against your *body of* **Sin** to save you from perishing *(John 3:16)*. Your *body of* **Sin** lusteth against God for itself. So, stop pretending to live as though you really know what the psalmist meant when he wrote *Psalms 23:1*. In *fact*, it is what *Psalms 23:1* says that awakens the **Sin** in our members and creates the problems we experience in our lives today and according *1John 1:8*, everyone has **Sin**. Just because you do not commit **Sins** does not mean that you do not have **Sin**. **Sinning** is a part of our nature; **Sins** are the actions of this nature. *Well Pastor, "What does Psalms 23:1 have to do with this"?* **Never say you do not want something**. To say you do not want something provokes the **Sin** nature in our earth suit to contend against the Word of God that we as believers were supposed to have hidden in our heart *(Psalms 119:11)*. Now please do not misunderstand me, God does want us to have the things of this world but He desires that we obtain them by faith. Satan wants you to try and obtain them through other means and for you to never live an un-contented life *(1Tim 6:6)*. So, while we keep quoting Psalms 23 saying, "*I shall not want*", Satan is saying, "*Yes you do*" and at the same **Time** daily tempting us to lust after the things we should not be lusting after. When we lust for the things of this world, they begin to draw us away from God and when lust hath conceived, it bringeth forth **Sin**: and **Sin**, when it is finished, bringeth forth **Death** *(James 1:14-15)*. Now, I am going to give you the benefit of the doubt and believe that you really *do not want*. However, *do you really not want*? Irregardless of what you might think or say, Satan will let God and others in the *body of Christ* know just how much *you really do not want*. How? He is going to vex and oppress you unto **Death** with the things you **Care** about. Let's read a few scripture verses about Samson and a lady named Delilah in *Judges 16:15-17*, they read,

"*And she said unto him, How canst thou say, I love thee, when thine heart is not with me? thou hast mocked me these three times, and hast not told me wherein thy great strength lieth. And it came to pass, when she pressed him **daily** with her words, and urged him, so that his soul was vexed unto **Death** That he told her all his heart, and said unto her. There hath not come a razor upon mine head; for I have been a Nazarite unto God from my mother's womb: if I be shaven, then my strength will go from me, and I shall become weak, and be like any other man.*"

Satan is going to show God, the heavenly host, the Body *of Christ (church)*, and the people of this world exactly **where your heart is and what's in it**? In the beginning of Samson's test, Samson did not tell Delilah where his strength lied (*I shall not want*). Therefore, because Samson *would not* tell her where his strength lied, she said "*How canst thou say, I love thee, when thine heart is not with me*". People hate when you mock them. Now, if you were to read the whole story about Samson, you would see that he had already mocked her twice in regards to where his strength lied. Well, God hates when you mock Him too. You better read *Galatians 6:7-8*. Now, look at verse 16, I underlined the word *daily*. Oh yeah, Satan is going to tempt you *daily* in order to break you and get you to comply with **Sin's** demands so that you can open a doorway for **Death** to enter your life. Why? Because you said, "*I shall not want*". People *do not want* to get divorced; people *do not want* to commit adultery; people *do not want* to kill and steal. Yet, they do. We also have born-again believers who after having received Christ as their life continue to commit these very same acts. When men say they *do not want*, **Sin** presses them *daily* for living obediently unto God by injecting evil thoughts and imaginations into their mind and when I say imaginations, these imaginations cannot be numbered. Please do not think for a second that Satan overcame Eve easily. Genesis 3, verses 1-6 records the conversation between the serpent and Eve, but I can assure you it took that serpent a lot of **Time** to overcome Eve and just as he deceived Eve, he is going to utilize some powerful imaginations to deceive you too. Imaginations that will paint your mind dark and make you see a future better than the future the Word of God paints for you. If you have ever painted something, then you know that dark paint covers light paint rather easily. Satan used some seriously dark paint on Eve's mind and he is doing this very same work on the minds of millions of humans today, including some born again believers. This dark paint that he uses has a name. It is called lies. His lies confuse us until we misinterpret the Word of God that was preached to you *(Hebrews 4:2)*. If he succeeds in his endeavors, he will paint your mind with so many lies until your mind is like paint sticking to the body of a car and it's going to take an accident to happen in your life before you can rid yourself of it. Did you know that people normally die in accidents? Remember what I wrote in the previous chapter, "**Sin** cannot die but we can". So, after Delilah *pressed Samson daily with her words, and urged him, so that his soul was vexed unto **Death**; he told her all his heart.* There it is. **Sin** is going to press you, urge you, and vex you *daily* until you give in to its demands. It does it by using dark evil thoughts and imaginations that the Word of God says in *2 Corinthians 10:5* that we are to cast down. Do you know what a thought is? A thought is a spoken word. In order for me to relay my thoughts to you, I must speak or write a word to you. What you are reading are my thoughts. Thoughts that I receiving from studying the Word of God.

Delilah was telling Samson her lust. Lust that were evil thoughts *(Gen 6:5)*. She definitely did not love him and just because they tell you that you do not love them does not mean that you have to submit to their evil, lustful thoughts and imaginations. Remember, *Sin* is Satan's nature and it is an evil nature. When the First Adam was made a living soul, he did not have a nature. He had the breath of life and with this life, God allowed him to choose the nature he wanted. He put two trees before the first man Adam to choose from. If *Sin* were the nature of the soul, then *Ezekiel 18:4 and 18:20* makes no sense. For they say, *"The soul that sinneth it shall die"*. The nature of the soul is not one laden with *Sin* but it can *Sin*. Now, *Romans 7:25* tells us that our earth suit is unified with this nature. The body of *Sin* that housed Samson finally wore him down from it's lust *(Gal 6:9)*.

Samson sinned, *"He told her all his heart"*. Why did Samson *Sin*. Samson had sin *(1John 1:8)*; He was born with a sinful nature. But, God had given him a word not to tell anyone where his strength lied. Oh, I can hear Satan questioning God, *"Does Samson fear you for naught, let me get next to him and I'll get him to tell a person the secret to where his strength lies"*. God had to do it; He doesn't fear anything, especially Satan. God believes and trust those men and women who say they love him to do just that, and it breaks His heart when we allow *Sin* to make a mockery of Him because God knows that there is nothing stronger in the life of a believer than His Word. Furthermore, God knows that whosoever it be that *Sins*, will suffer ***Death***. No parent wants to see their children die. So, they teach them about the dangers of life. Samson's parents trained him and taught him about what the Word of God said concerning his hair. But instead of loving this gift from God, Samson fell to Delilah's temptations, ***Caring*** more about her desires than God's desires.

Everyone has good desires. If Satan can get them to think about or look at something, by nature, they will desire it. This desire is normal behavior. The problem arises when the desire is forbidden by God. Therefore, Satan *daily* tempts men them to look at and think about the forbidden or harmful thing more than they should. If this happens, they begin to lust after it. This is the very beginning stage of temptation. Samson began to play with Delilah. Satan deceived him until he failed to realize that he was spending too much **Time** focusing upon playing games with her. So, while he was playing with her, Satan was using Delilah to vex him <u>*daily*</u>. After Samson's temptations became too much for him to bear, Samson told her the secret to where his strength lied and she cut off his hair. When she cut off his hair, it opened a doorway for **Death** to destroy his strength. What is **Death**? **Death** is inability. After Samson told her all his heart, *she made him sleep upon her knees; and she called for a man, and <u>she caused him to shave off the seven locks of his head</u>; and she began to afflict him, and <u>his strength went from him</u>. And she said, The Philistines be upon thee, Samson. And he awoke out of his sleep, and said, I will go out as at other times before, and shake myself. <u>And he wist not that the Lord was departed from him</u>.*

When Samson sinned, the Lord departed from him. After the Lord left Samson, he was no longer able *(inability)* to defeat the Philistines *as at other times* and they brought **Death** into several areas of his life, beginning with his eyesight. **Sin** will use **Death** to take away those things you **Care** about and handicap you. **Sin** turned Samson into a handicapped **Man of God** *(John 9:2)*. How was **Sin** able to handicap Samson? Let's read <u>*Romans 6:23*</u>, it says,

*"For the wages of **Sin** is **Death**; but the gift of God is eternal life through Jesus Christ our Lord."*

Sin gave Samson his wages. Wages that went to his strength and eyesight. Do you know what wages are? Wages is money received for work done. It would be evil of somebody to say they will pay you wages for the work you do for them and not pay you for doing those wages. ***Death*** is the wages men receive after they ***Sin***. Samson rented his hair to Delilah, a gentile, true servant of ***Sin***, an enemy of Israel, and a citizen of the world.

Let's see it from another view point. If you are a rental agency and you rent out equipment to the customer, you rent it to that customer and they pay you wages for renting it to them. God gave Samson his hair. Samson rented his hair out to the Philistines. Samson was not supposed to let the philistines know what God had done for him because they were God's enemies. When he rented them his hair, they gave him wages of ***Death*** to his eyesight.

Let's not look down on Samson. We have ***Sin*** too *(1John 1:8)*. If you say you have no ***Sin***, you are deceiving yourself. Your earth suit is *the body of **Sin***. The wages owed to your earth suit is ***Death***. Now, the wages God gives to the soul is ***Time***. The wages the soul receives for believing in His only begotten Son is everlasting life. However, the soul that refuses to believe in His only begotten son remains united with their *body of **Sin***; a body that is due to receive wages of ***Death***. When ***Time*** expires on the earth suit *(Hebrews 9:27)*, it will receive wages of ***Death*** and ***Death*** corrupts it *(Gen 3:19)*. The soul does not die, but sleeps until the day of judgment. On this day, it will be judged *(2Cor 5:10)*.

Notice, God did not allow Samson's ***Sin*** to take his life. It is God who Samson sinned against, not Satan. Samson's disobedience to the Word of God allowed ***Sin*** to bring ***Death*** to his liberty, his joy, and his eyesight but not his life. Now do you see, ***Death*** encompasses more than just the end of a person's life. Let's read *Romans 7:20*, it says,

*"Now if I do that I would not, it is no more I that do it, but **Sin** that dwelleth in me"*.

This is ***Man's Dilemma***. Every human has ***Sin*** dwelling in them. The forerunner of ***Death***. Men want to do the will of

God, but **Sin** contends with men every **Time** they strive to do the will of God. The first man Adam received a life from the Lord God that knew no **Sin** and a Body and both lusted against the other *(Gal 5:17)*. How do I know this? Well if this were not true, then why did the LORD God Adam, "*Of every tree of the garden thou mayest freely eat; But of the tree of the knowledge of good and evil, thou shalt not eat of it: for in the day that thou eatest thereof thou shalt surely die (Genesis 2:16-17).*"

Now, I cannot say that the first man Adam lusted after the forbidden tree but I can say that Eve did. All I know is that Adam willfully ate from the tree. When he ate from that tree, all types of evil imaginations spouted within his heart; imaginations that have been passed on to all men through our *body of Sin*. And *Genesis 6:5* says, "*That every imagination of the thoughts of man's heart was only evil **continually**".*

That is our **Dilemma**. We have continual evil knowledge traveling with us everywhere we go. Christ, the last Adam was not subject to this knowledge. In *Phil 2:6-8* Christ Jesus, subjected Himself to and clothed himself in a *body of Sin* but He did not **Sin** according to *Rom 6:12 & 13:14*. Why? Christ was not carnally minded. **Flesh** and blood born men are and it is this canal mindedness that triggers us to lust for any and everything. Lust that prevent our eyes from ever being satisfied and when it is not satisfied, all forms of evil knowledge *(Prov 27:20)* arise from our hearts. This is probably why the Philistine's blinded Samson. For I am sure they knew in their heart that Samson's desire to destroy them would never be satisfied if he regained his hair and could visibly see them. So, make sure you understand the meaning behind, "*I shall not want*" before you say it because **Sin** is waiting for you to say those words so it can make you out to be a liar before God and the world. And, again I say, you do have **Sin**. *1John 1:8* says,

"*If we say that we have no **Sin**, we deceive ourselves, and the truth is not in us*".

We have **Sin** and when you come to realize that you cannot resist its demands, you need to start looking for someone who can. God has given us someone who can. His name is Christ Jesus, the Son of the Living God, the last Adam. The Apostle James tells us in *James 5:19-20,* that our **belief** in Him will save our soul's from **Death** and hide a multitude of **Sins**. Let's look at *1 John 5:11-13*. These verses read,

> *"And this is the record, that God hath given to us eternal life, and this life is in his Son. <u>He that hath the Son hath life; and he that hath not the Son of God hath not life. These things have I written unto you that believe on the name of the Son of God;</u> that ye may know that ye have eternal life, and that ye may believe on the name of the Son of God."*

It does not say that, *"He who keeps the law hath life"*, it says, *"He that hath the Son hath life"*. Also, *John 3:15-20* says,

> *"That whosoever believeth in him should not perish, but have eternal life. For God so loved the world, that he gave his only begotten Son, that whosoever believeth in him should not perish, but have everlasting life. For God sent not his Son into the world to condemn the world; but that the world through him might be saved. He that believeth on him is not condemned: but he that believeth not is condemned already, because he hath not believed in the name of the only begotten Son of God. And this is the condemnation, that light is come into the world, and men loved darkness rather than light, because their deeds were evil. For every one that doeth evil hateth the light, neither cometh to the light, lest his deeds should be reproved."*

When God gave the world his son, the law of **Sin** and **Death** was active. In **fact**, it was the law keepers who crucified Christ Jesus. Why? *1Cor 15:56*, tells us that *the law is the strength of* **Sin**. These law keepers killed Christ Jesus because he exposed their deeds in *John 8:36-45*. Now, 2000 years after Christ has risen from the dead, men preach messages from *the oldness of the letter* unto servants of righteousness *(Romans 6:17-18)*.

Ministries that minister on these grounds are causing a lot of confusion in the *Body of Christ* and caused many of God's children to err in their faith. Now, I know for a *fact* that when Christ died for the lost, it was not so that those in the ministry would confuse them. Furthermore, I definitely know for a *fact* that it is not the words of Jesus causing the confusion. Men and women who have been baptized in Jesus name and walk in newness of life in the Spirit are delivered from this world and the curses that apply to those who refuse to reject its ways *(Lev 10:1-2)*. Once a person receives Christ as Lord and Savior of their life, they become Sons of God and walk by the faith that comes from hearing, and hearing by the Word of God *(Romans 10:17)*. Furthermore, those who believe in God's Word, God accounts their belief as righteousness. Let's read *Mark 16:16*. It says,

"He that believeth and is baptized shall be saved; but he that believeth not shall be damned."

He that believeth what? In Jesus and is baptized in his name *(Acts 2:38, Romans 10:9-13, John 6:28-29)*. The man or woman who obeys this principle shall be saved. How simpler can this verse be written. The problem in the church today is that people think that the *sayings and teachings* of Jesus saves a person from *Hell*. No, it saves them from the world. Lord, let me write that again. ***The problem in the church today is that people think that the sayings and teachings of Jesus saves a person from Hell. No, it saves them from the world.*** Nobody says this better than the Apostle John. In *1John 2:15-17*, he tells us,

"Love not the world, neither the things that are in the world. If any man love the world, the love of the Father is not in him. For all that is in the world, the lust of the flesh, and the lust of the eyes, and the pride of life, is not of the Father, but is of the world. And the world passeth away, and the lust thereof: but he that doeth the will of God abideth for ever."

Why should we not love the world? Satan is the God of this world, this world is filled with violence and hatred, and God is going to destroy it with Satan and all the fallen angels who rebelled against God with him. If you do not escape this world and the lust of it, you will perish with Satan and anyone who is friends with this world. Let me illustrate. *If you are in an airplane, high in the sky and it blows up, what are your chances of survival? Zero.* Now, listen to what John 3:16-17 says. It says,

"For God so loved the world, that he gave his only begotten Son, that whosoever believeth in him should not perish, but have everlasting life. For God sent not his Son into the world to condemn the world; but that the world through him might be saved."

It is only through Jesus *that the world through him might be saved* and that men *should not perish*. If you do not **believe** this, you are damned *(Mark 16:16)*. If you **believe** this and get baptized, God accounts your **belief** as righteousness. Furthermore, Abraham's belief in the Word of God is proof that God counts our belief in Him as righteousness (*Romans 4:3)* and according to *Matthew 22:32* which says, *"I am the God of Abraham, and the God of Isaac, and the God of Jacob? God is not the God of the dead, but of **the living**"*. Abraham *did not perish* nor is he said to be dead. Why? Because he believed God. This same principles applies to every born again man or woman who believes the *sayings and teachings* of Jesus. Who is Jesus? He is the Word made **Flesh** *(John 1:14)*. Let's talk water baptism to see the importance of it and what it symbolizes in the life of a believer. *Genesis 6: 11-13* says,

"The earth also was corrupt before God, and the earth was filled with violence. And God looked upon the earth, and, behold, it was corrupt; for all flesh had corrupted his way upon the earth. And God said unto Noah, The end of all flesh is come before me; for the earth is filled with violence through them; and, behold, I will destroy them with the earth."

The entire earth is corrupt. Who corrupted it? The first man Adam, Satan, and **Sin**. The first man Adam's transgression

87

enabled Satan to become the God of this world. Now, Satan and the third of the angels *(Rev 12:3-4)* that were cast out of heaven *(Jude 6)* have corrupted the earth through the power of a law called **Sin**. The earth we live on today has been and is being corrupted by principalities, powers, rulers of the darkness of this world, and spiritual wickedness in high places *(Eph 6:12)* and there is nothing men can do about it apart from the Word of God *(John 15:5)*. Why? Because God gave the earth to mankind for men to have dominion over it and Satan leaves God no other choice but to destroy it because of the law of **Sin** that rules it. So now, because of the first man Adam's transgression, **Sin** now governs the life of men and it keeps men separated from God *(Isaiah 59:2)*. **Sin** causes *all **Flesh** to corrupt its way upon the earth.* The **Flesh** of men and of beast. Yes, beast too. The serpent sinned too; it surrendered its body to Satan first. *Genesis 3:1-5* says,

"*Now the serpent was more subtil than any beast of the field which the LORD God had made. And he said unto the woman, Yea, hath God said, Ye shall not eat of every tree of the garden? And the woman said unto the serpent, We may eat of the fruit of the trees of the garden: But of the fruit of the tree which is in the midst of the garden, God hath said, Ye shall not eat of it, neither shall ye touch it, lest ye die. And the serpent said unto the woman, Ye shall not surely die: For God doth know that in the day ye eat thereof, then your eyes shall be opened, and ye shall be as gods, knowing good and evil.*"

The serpent yielded its body to Satan first. Moses tells us in *Genesis 1:25,* that when God created the beast of the field, *He saw that it was good.* There was a **Time** when men and beast were good. However, after the first man Adam fell, the LORD God cursed the ground for Adam's sake. The ground is where all animals proceedeth from *(Gen 1:24)*. What made these animals un-good? Satan, the Devil. Through the use of the man and beasts cursed bodies, Satan is now able to go to and fro in the earth (***mode of transportation***), walking up and down in it as told in *Job 1:7*; corrupting it with great wrath *(Rev 12:12)*. Therefore, God decided to destroy *the earth because it was filled* *with violence through man and beasts' bodies of **Sin***. Don't let this upset you, God thought of a way to save mankind. A plan called baptism. By baptism, man by believing and having faith *(Heb 11:7)* in water baptism, could experience **Death** and walk in newness of life *(Romans 6:4)* through the operation of the Holy Spirit. Now, let's read *Genesis 6:17* and see how God would carry out this plan. It reads,

"And, behold, I, even I, do bring a flood of waters upon the earth, to destroy all flesh, wherein is the breath of life, from under heaven; and every thing that is in the earth shall die."

The plan required the coming together of water and earth. A plan that would restore things as they were before men fell. A plan that returns the earth to its original place in creation; a place where the earth is completely submerged under water *(Gen 1:9)*. Therefore, when a human believes *Jesus' teachings and sayings* about water baptism *(John 3:5)* and is baptized in His name, that person in the eyes of God has tasted **Death** and is raised by the Spirit in newness of life. Let me explain it to you the way God explained it to me. *Genesis 1:9-10* says,

"And God said, <u>Let the waters under the heaven be gathered together unto one place, and let the dry land appear:</u> and it was so. And God called the dry land Earth; and the gathering together of the waters called he Seas: and God saw that it was good."

When a person obeys the *teachings and sayings of Jesus* and receives immersion under water in Jesus name, God counts it as dry land appearing from under the waters that are gathered together unto one place. This leads me to believe that water baptism involves the complete immersion of our earthen vessels and not a sprinkling (*I hope some of the ministries who have not completely immersed your members in water rebaptize those members*). No where in the bible will you see God instructing anyone to sprinkle water, only blood. God completely baptized Noah and his family in the Ark *(Gen 7:7-10)*. In *Exodus 14:22*, He completely baptized the Children of Israel in the Red Sea. In

Joshua 3:17, He completely baptized those who were allowed to pass over the River Jordan into the Promised Land. In *2 Kings 2:6-15*, we see the baptism of Elijah and Elisha in the Jordan. I find it odd that we have theologians who cannot teach people this simple principle. Isn't it strange how every adult ought to know that when a child is in the womb of its mother, that it is immersed in water. Now, I see why Jesus told His disciples in *Matthew 18:3*, *"Except ye be converted, and become as little children, ye shall not enter into the kingdom of heaven"* and in *John 3:6*, *"That which is born of the flesh is flesh; and that which is born of the Spirit is spirit."*

As men are born into this world, their birth occurred as a result of the will of the **Flesh** and everyone born of the will of the **Flesh** is born in the image and likeness of the first man Adam *(Gen 5:3)*. After the first man Adam and Eve sinned, their nature and last name, in which I will call sinner, became every person's nature and last name. By nature, they are sinners and so are we. How? By **one blood**. However, in *Genesis 1:26-27* the first man Adam was born of the Will of the Father. This man's blood lacked the knowledge of good and evil *(Gen 3:22)* and because of that, **Sin** did not have dominion over him nor could **Death** corrupt or hold him *(Acts 2:24)*. But, the first man Adam fell and **Sin** has made our earthen vessel Its *habitation* and now that it governs our body, it is able to oppress our souls to obey it. However, **Sin** can only use the things of this world to do this oppression. Furthermore, Jesus in *John 6:63* says, *"It is the spirit that quickeneth; the flesh profiteth nothing: **the words that I speak unto you, they are spirit, and they are life**."*

The words Jesus speaks **are spirit, and they are life**. Not the words Moses speaks, or the fathers speak. Jesus Only. It was Jesus who told us that we should be baptized *(Mark 16:16)*. Now, if it was Jesus who instructed us to be baptized of water and we get baptized of water, then who was it that baptized us. Was it our Pastors and ministers who baptized us or was it our Pastors and ministers obedience and submission to *Jesus' saying sand teachings* that **are spirit, and life** which baptizes believers. If we say that it was *Jesus' sayings and teachings*, then not only are we born of the water by being immersed under it but also of the Spirit since it was *Jesus' Words* that commands Pastors and ministers to do it *(James 1:22)*.

The Words Jesus spoke while on the earth were God's Words, and in *John 4:24,* He tells us that God is a Spirit. These are the same words that tell us how to obtain rebirth, God's way. A way paved by faith; the faith spoken of in *Hebrews 11:1, 6*. When we live by faith and in obedience to the Words spoken by the Holy Spirit that believers receive after repentance and water baptism *(Acts 2:38)*. Whosoever it be that obeys these instructions *(2Tim 3:16)*, makes it impossible for **Death** to hold them *(Acts 2:24)*. Something that we as believers should have read about in *Acts 2:24.* Believers need to know that they are now filled with Christ as their life *(Col 3:4)*. If you do not believe what I just explained or in the baptism of Jesus Christ, you will die cursed *(Genesis 3:17)* in this world and according to *Mark 16:16*, are damned already.

Unbelief in the word of God places every man, male or female, in a position to be damned to **Death.** Man's earth suit was judged in Genesis, Chapter 3, not man's soul. Man's soul was allowed to live **(Samson and King David too)**. Why? So that the soul may continue to corrupt the earth and rebel against the Lord with its *body of Sin*. NO!!! The soul was allowed to live because *2Peter 3:9-15* tells us that the Lord loves man and has no desire to see men perish. God's will for mankind is for men to live eternally with Him and His Son Christ Jesus; for me to occupy the new earth he has prepared for those who love him, keep his commandments, and remain faithful unto **Death** as foretold in *Rev 2:10*.

This message, the message of the Gospel, is what God has been trying to get men to receive and **believe** since the beginning of **Time**. Yet, men do not **believe** it and their unbelief is keeping them as slaves to **Sin** and a world that will end in **Death**. If it were not for unbelief, **Sin** would not be able to control you nor would you or I receive wages unto **Death**. The only wages we would receive would be wages overflowing with everlasting life *(John 3:16)*.

Nevertheless, there are millions of humans still living carnal mindedly in the *Flesh* who have heard this Gospel message. A message that believers have been preaching over and over again for more than 2000 years but men refuse to *believe* the truths of it *(Prov 29:1)*. It was Noah's *belief* in God that saved him and his family from *Death*, not the flood. Why? Noah had the keys *(Faith)*. It was Lot's *belief* in God that saved him and his family from the *Death* of fire and brimstone, not Sodom and Gomorrah. *2Pet 2:7-8* tells us that Lot had the keys *(Faith,)* even though Mrs. Lot *Cared* for the things of those cities *(world)* than God's salvation plan for her. *Belief* in God delivered the children of Israel from slavery in Egypt and saved them from the *Death* of the last plaque pronounced on the first born children of Egypt. Why? Moses had the keys *(Faith)* and they believed the words he preached unto them. *Belief* in God saved the three Hebrew boys mentioned in Daniel, chapter three from the *Death* of Nebuchadnezzar's fiery furnace. Why? Because of their *Faith* in the Word of God, not the Law. It was their obedience to the law that put them in that predicament but it was their *Faith* and their fear of disobeying the commandments of the LORD God that delivered them from the fiery furnace and because of their *Faith*, Nebuchadnezzar made a decree in *Dan 3:29*, that every people, nation, and language, which spoke any thing amiss against the God of Shadrach, Meshach, and Abed-nego, shall be cut in pieces, and their houses shall be made a dunghill: because there is no other God that can deliver after this sort. Now, the soldiers that threw them into the fire encountered *Death*, because they did not believe in the God of the Hebrew boys and they didn't even go into the furnace they only felt the flames from it.

Remember what I said earlier concerning *2Peter 3:9.* The Lords will is for all men to be delivered from the power of *Death*. *Death* of the spirit, *Death* of the soul, and *Death* of the body. But men continue to allow *Sin* to hold them in its grasp living life as though they do not want to be delivered. Nevertheless, I **believe** that they want to be delivered. However, they are having a hard *Time* locating a true man or woman of God that will not cater to their **Sinful** lifestyle or evil communication *(arguments)* when they need to be reproved but continue feed them the Word of God without measure regardless of their carnal tantrums. But sadly, they cannot find one who exhibits this character trait and are left to sit under ministries that teach them after the manner of the Law and its commandments. I say this because I was one of these people. I was once a member of a church whose teachings kept born again believers mindful of earthly things which all are to perish with the using after the commandments and doctrines of men? Which things indeed have a shew of wisdom *in will worship*, and humility, and neglecting of the body; not in any honour to the satisfying of the **Flesh** *(Col 2:22-23)*.

God desires that we worship him in spirit and in truth, not *will worship*. God desires that we walk in the spirit; walk with the mind of Christ, and live in the spirit. Our *will worship* has to do with the self life. The life that we are to reckon as dead. If you do not reckon this life as dead, if you do not hate your life that you received at birth, then you will lose it. John 12:25 says, *"He that loveth his life shall **lose it**; and he that hateth his life in this world shall keep it unto life eternal."* if you continue to live your life unrepentant, and unbaptized, and you die in your **Sin**s then at **Death**, when you lie in your grave, it will be like a dungeon to you and according to *Job 20:11* which says,

"His bones are full of the Sin of his youth, which shall lie down with him in the dust".

Then not only will **Death** be the holding cell for your dust, it will hold the **Sins** of your youth as well and on Judgment Day, when you are resurrected, you and your **Sins together**, shall appear before the judgment seat of Christ; that you may receive the things done in your body, according to that you hath done, whether it be good or bad *(2Cor 5:10)*. I do not know what your judgment will be, I am not God. But you do because you know what you do and whose *sayings and teachings* you obey. Do you obey the lust of your earth suit or *Jesus' sayings*? Do you still rely on the teachings of the law to justify that if you obey them that they will position you in right standing with God?

Some people who hear me preach think I hate the law. They think I preach that the law should not be kept. I do not hate the law and the commandments. I hate ministers who do not know how to teach it *(Romans 9:13, Matt 5:20)*. Moses gave the law and the commandments to the children of Israel. However, *Gal 3:21* tells us that those laws could not give life. I only have one word for law keepers and their followers *(Matthew 15:14)*, as long as you continue believing that the law can give a man life and justify them before God by submitting themselves to its teachings and not *Jesus' teachings or sayings*, you will end up teaching those who are partakers of life another gospel; something to which Paul warnings the Galatian church about in *Gal 1:8-9*. As teachers of God, you need to know that all a believer has to do in order to please God is live *John 6:28-29* and apply *James 4:7-8* to their life. *James 4:7-8* says,

"*Submit yourselves therefore to God. Resist the devil, and he will flee from you. Draw nigh to God, and he will draw nigh to you. Cleanse your hands, ye sinners; and purify your hearts, ye double minded.*"

James in his letter says; *cleanse your hands, ye sinners*. All men are sinners *(Gal 2:15-17)*. However, we are not to cleanse our hands the way Pilate cleansed his hands *(Matthew 27:22-24)*. *1Tim 2:8* instructs believers to *cleanse their hands and lift up holy hands, without wrath and doubting.* James also instructs us to, *Submit to God*, not the law *and purify your hearts, ye double minded.* The reason he instructs in this manner is because in *James 1:8* he warned that a double minded man is unstable in all his ways. Either submit to God *(Spirit)* or serve the law *(Letter) (2Cor 3:6)*. If you are a professing Christian, you should be walking with the mind of Christ, not a double mind. Not a mind mixed with Old and New Testament doctrines. Why? Because of what Jesus taught His disciples in *Luke 5:37-38*. He says,

*"No man putteth **new wine** into old bottles; else the new wine will burst the bottles, and be spilled, and the bottles shall perish. But **new wine** must be put into new bottles; and both are preserved."*

Do not let anyone put Old Covenant teachings into your New Covenant life *(1Tim 1:8-11)*. You are a new creature in Christ Jesus *(2Cor 5:17)*. We receive our instructions for living from the preaching of the Gospel. Look at what *Hebrews 4:2* says. It says,

"For unto us was the gospel preached, as well as unto them: but the word preached did not profit them, not being mixed with faith in them that heard it."

Ministers of the New Testament should only be preaching about life in the spirit *(2Cor 3:6)*. A life that returns us unto God which delivers men from **Death**. The gospel of Jesus Christ and his life is the message that should be heard in the world today, not a message from the Law, even though it was good but it could not give life. It is very easy to see a lot of churches still mixing the law with faith. This makes me wonder if they have ever read *Romans 3:31*. It says, *"Do we then make void the law through **faith**? God forbid: yea, we establish the law."* We do not void the law; by faith we establish it. That is why I do not hate it. People who teach believers that they must keep the law cause them to give attention to the **Flesh** thereby creating a war in that believer's mind who has chosen to serve the Law of God *(Spirit)* as mentioned in *Romans 7:25* and not the letter.

I know so many people who want to be delivered from this world. Yet, because they have not dealt with the issue of their earth suit *(Matt 16:24, Mark 8:34, Luke 9:23)*, they remain in bondage to **Sin**. This is why the teaching on water baptism is so important in the life of a believer but water baptism did not come from the Old Testament. Water baptisms however, were performed in the Old Testament but not in Jesus name. It was done by an act of the Word of God. No human before John the

Baptist physically immersed anyone, God did it by and through His Word. Therefore, through the participation of water baptism and rebirth of the spirit by the washing of regeneration as mentioned in *Titus 3:5*, believers receive and possess everything they need in life at the *Time* of regeneration. A life that replaces the life we received from the first man Adam. Nevertheless, *Sin* will not let you go that easily. When you accept Christ as Lord and Savior of your life, Satan and those third of angels will begin to wage an all out war against your soul in order to regain control of you. They will do everything they can to reenter your life and hold you in bondage to *Sin*'s controlling power. Let's look at *2 Cor 10:3-6* which says,

"For though we walk in the flesh, we do not war after the flesh: (For the weapons of our warfare are not carnal, but mighty through God to the pulling down of strong holds;) Casting down imaginations, and every high thing that exalteth itself against the knowledge of God, and bringing into captivity every thought to the obedience of Christ; And having in a readiness to revenge all disobedience, when your obedience is fulfilled."

Even though we are baptized, we still walk in this *Flesh*, no doubt about that but we do not war after it. Meaning we do not *Care* for it or what it lust and desires to obtain. Still, Satan and those fallen angels do not believe this. Let's look at *Luke 11:24-26* that says,

"When the unclean spirit is gone out of a man, he walketh through dry places, seeking rest, and findeth none. Then he saith, I will return into my house from whence I came out; and when he is come, he findeth it empty, swept, and garnished. Then goeth he, and taketh with himself seven other spirits more wicked than himself, and they enter in and dwell there: and the last state of that man is worse than the first."

Satan is coming. That's why it is vital that you purchase a good commentary, find yourself a true man or woman of God and ask them to expound on *Romans 6:3-23* for you. These verses say,

Know ye not, that so many of us as were baptized into Jesus Christ were baptized into his death? [4] Therefore we are buried with him by baptism into death: that like as Christ was raised up from the dead by the glory of the Father, even so we also should walk in newness of life. *[5] For if we have been planted together in the likeness of his death, we shall be also in the likeness of his resurrection: [6] **Knowing this, that our old man is crucified with him, that the body of sin might be destroyed, that henceforth we should not serve sin**. [7] For he that is dead is freed from sin. [8] Now if we be dead with Christ, we believe that we shall also live with him: [9] Knowing that Christ being raised from the dead dieth no more; death hath no more dominion over him. [10] For in that he died, he died unto sin once: but in that he liveth, he liveth unto God. [11] Likewise reckon ye also yourselves to be dead indeed unto sin, but alive unto God through Jesus Christ our Lord. [12] Let not sin therefore reign in your mortal body, that ye should obey it in the lusts thereof. [13] Neither yield ye your members as instruments of unrighteousness unto sin: but yield yourselves unto God, as those that are alive from the dead, and your members as instruments of righteousness unto God. [14] For sin shall not have dominion over you: for ye are not under the law, but under grace. [15] What then? shall we sin, because we are not under the law, but under grace? God forbid. [16] Know ye not, that to whom ye yield yourselves servants to obey, his servants ye are to whom ye obey; whether of sin unto death, or of obedience unto righteousness? [17] But God be thanked, that ye were the servants of sin, but ye have obeyed from the heart that form of doctrine which was delivered you. [18] Being then made free from sin, ye became the servants of righteousness. [19] I speak after the manner of men because of the infirmity of your flesh: for as ye have yielded your members servants to uncleanness and to iniquity unto iniquity; even so now yield your members servants to righteousness unto holiness. [20] For when ye were the servants of sin, ye were free from righteousness. [21] What fruit had ye then in those things whereof ye are now ashamed?*

for the end of those things is death. [22] But now being made free from sin, and become servants to God, ye have your fruit unto holiness, and the end everlasting life. [23] For the wages of sin is death; but the gift of God is eternal life through Jesus Christ our Lord.

Oh, if believers would meditate on these verses and hearken unto *Jesus' sayings and teachings* and get an understanding of His word *(Job 34:16, Prov 4:5, Eph 1:18)* about water baptism. Because when a person is baptized, in the eyes of God, your Adamic natured man is dead and buried. There is nothing that can move a person out of this world faster than **Death**. Water baptism buries men into Christ's **Death** *(Rom 6:3)*. Once a person is baptized in Jesus name, it is like putting them into a tomb and burying them. This burial separates them from the world. They are now Dead to this world and the rudiments of it. A world that the Apostle John in *1John 5:19* says, "*lieth in wickedness.*" My prayer is that you will begin to study the Word of God and allow the Spirit of God lead you to a real man or woman of God and that you will submit yourself to the teachings. Why? Because if you are not delivered from this world and you die *(Remember what I said about the airplane blowing up)*, on Judgment Day, when you are resurrected, you and your **Sins** will stand before God and be judged *(Rev 20: 12-13)*. Believers and unbelievers may not agree on a lot of things, but there is one thing that we all agree on. We agree that **Death** is a reality. The first Adam brought **Death** into the world and passed it unto all men. Christ Jesus' **Death** on the cross frees us from the power of Death *(Acts 2:24)*. The soul that believes this and is baptized is buried with Christ into **Death**: that like as Christ was raised from **Death** by the glory of the Father, even so shall the believer be raised from **Death** *(1Cor 15:55)*. Without a doubt all **Flesh** will experience **Death**. The life passed to us from the first Adam must experience it in order to mortify the **Sin** mingled in it. Therefore, my prayer like Paul's prayer was for Israel *(Romans 10:1-2)* is that all men will experience the **Death** plan of God before you experience the **Death** sentence passed unto us through the life of the first Adam *(Rom 5:15)*. There is nothing mysterious about God's great salvation plan for mankind. Every human has and will hear about it but many will refuse to believe it. So, in closing this chapter, I will write *Mark 16:16* once again, it reads, "***He or she that believeth in this plan, shall be saved; but he or she that believeth not shall be damned***.

HELL

*He seeing this before spake of the resurrection of Christ, that his soul was not left in **Hell**, neither his flesh did see corruption.*
Acts 2:31

Due to some of the sermons preached in numerous church services today and movies filmed in the Hollywood studios, the consciences of men, including some born again believers, has been seared *(1Tim 4:1-2)* with lies and this searing has many people believing they know what **Hell** is and who resides there after **Death**. Nevertheless, even in the midst of all this confusion, the Word of God gives undisputable truths of who abides within the gates of **Hell** *(Matt 16:18/Jude 6)*. Let me give you a clue. It isn't the first man Adam imaged person.

Now, before I speak on this subject, a foundation **must** be laid in order for you to get a good understanding of **Hell**. First, **Hell** is not of this world. The first man Adam imaged person is of this world. **Hell**, is a spiritual world, a world on the other side of **Death**. The LORD prepared it as a *temporary holding cell* for the disobedient one's who were in a covenant relationship with him; individuals who are or were spiritually connected to God. Yes, **Hell** is a temporary place, I know what I wrote.

In the beginning, when mankind was created, neither God nor the Lord God mentioned this world to the first man Adam and Eve, only Heaven and Earth are mentioned. It wasn't until **Sin** entered the world that men needed knowledge concerning this world. Why? Because of a new birth experience men were about to learn about from God. The first Adam's transgression in the Garden of Eden passed **Death** unto all men. If it were not for **Death**, we would not need any knowledge of this world. But, now that we know **Death**, our relationship with God's Son requires that we come to know about **Hell** also.

In creation, the only world God meant for men to know about was a world that consisted of life on planet earth void of **Death**. So, in the first two chapters of Genesis, The Godhead that's mentioned in <u>Genesis 1:26 / 1John 5:7</u>, created a world for mankind to dwell in, created a planet that He named, Earth and formed the man an earth suit out of it.

In this world, the LORD God planted a garden eastward in Eden; and there he put the man whom he had formed in <u>Genesis 2:8</u>. However, In this garden dwelt two trees. Through these two trees, the first man Adam would determine the type of world mankind would live in. He was given the choice of choosing a world filled with **Life and Peace** or a world filled with **Good, Evil, and Death**. As you can see, the first Adam chose the world filled with Good, Evil, and **Death**.

Now, God knew that if the first man Adam ate from the forbidden tree, every human would be born into this world with a life full of Good, Evil, **Death**; a life mingled with **Sin** that would oppress men and cause them to rebel against the will of God for our lives. Therefore, in <u>1Peter 1:20 & Rev 13:8</u> the word of God tells us that before our world was founded, God slew and sent His Son to be the propitiation of our sins. An act of God known through out the church today as God's great salvation plan for man. A plan that involved God, His Son, and the Holy Spirit. A plan which declares that if a man or woman believed on the name of God's only begotten Son, Christ Jesus, that they would be delivered from this present evil world and **Death** as promised in <u>Gal 1:4& John 5:24,1John 3:14</u>. Let's begin this chapter.

Any man or woman who accepts Christ Jesus as Lord and Savior of their life and lives obediently to His Words, God has promised to give them eternal life. But, with this life comes a knowledge of two new worlds. <u>Mark 9:47 & Eph 5:5</u> tells us that one of these worlds is called "*the kingdom of God*" and <u>Mark 9:43-47</u> calls the other world, <u>**Hell**</u>. In <u>Luke 9:27, John 3:5</u> we are told that the man or woman who accepts Christ Jesus as Lord and Savior of their life, and obey <u>His sayings or teachings</u>, shall receive everlasting life and enter into the Kingdom of God when they die. Contrariwise, the man or woman who accepts Christ Jesus as the Lord and Savior of their life but continue to disobey *His sayings or teachings*, and become the servants of **Sin** once again, shall enter into **Hell** when they die just as the rich man did in *Luke 16:22-25*.

Now in *Luke 16:22-23*, The Bible gives us some insight on **Hell**. It shows us that Hell is a *holding cell for the disobedient who are in a covenant relationship with God but do not obey the sayings or teachings of Christ Jesus or who do not love the brethren but experience physical* **Death** *before Christ raptures the church out of this world as promised in 1Thes 4:16-17.* Let's read *John 5:24*, it reads,

*"Verily, verily, I say unto you, He that heareth my word, and believeth on him that sent me, hath everlasting life, and shall not come into condemnation; but is **passed from death unto life**."*

Once a man or woman believes in Christ Jesus and is baptized in His name as instructed in *Acts 2:38*, that believer receives the gift of the Holy Ghost and *shall not come into condemnation (Romans 8:1); but is **passed from Death unto life**.* Why? First, *Gal 3:27* tells us that *"the believer that has been baptized into Christ, has taken off the first man Adam life and put on Christ."* Second, water baptism in Jesus name buries the first man Adam image man in **Death**, thereby killing the sinful self life that all men are born with *(Matt 10:39)*. Let's read *Romans 6:4* again. It reads, *"Therefore we are buried with him by baptism into **Death**."* Water baptism buries men into **Death**. Now, I'll let you answer this next question for yourself. If you are buried in **Death**, how can you experience **Death** again when you are already in it? By Faith, Men are buried into **Death** through water baptism and this burial *passes them from death unto life (Gal 3:26-29)*. Water baptism to the soul mirrors what the Ark was to Noah. Water baptism buries our first man Adam image life unto **Death** and passes our soul through **Death** and unto life; through the **Death** caused by the **Sin** of the first man Adam enabling us to walk in the newness of life. A new life that believers may now enter into the Kingdom of God with according to what Jesus said in *John 3:5*. Likewise, the Ark passed Noah through the **Death** of the flood so that he, his family, and all those animals could walk in the newness of life in a new world void of all the **Sinfulness** they previously had to endure. Water baptism, the Flood, the Ark, **Death** and **Sin**, the first man Adam, Noah, and his family are of this world. A world that lieth in wickedness according to *1John 5:19;* a world corrupted by **Sin** and **Death**. **Hell** is not so. It is not of this world and whatever enters its gates does not corrupt *(Die)* but is tormented like the rich man in *Luke 16:24-25*. True worshippers of God *(John 4:23-24)*, you need not worry about **Death** or **Hell** because the life of Christ that you received at water baptism and because you've *remained faithful unto **Death***, transcends **Death** as well as the world of **Hell**. The Bible says in *Acts 2:31* that,

"*He seeing this before spake of the resurrection of Christ, that **his soul was not left in Hell**, neither **his flesh did see corruption (Death)**.*"

Jesus' obedience to the Word of God and His *faithfulness unto Death* made a way for God to highly exalt him, and give a name which is above every name and whom God hath also made both Lord and Christ *(Phil 2:9)*. Christ's willingness to live faithful to His Father God, ensured that **His soul was not left in Hell, nor did His Flesh see corruption/Death (Please read Luke 24:1-53)**. Believers, your faithfulness to God will do the same for you.

"*Well Pastor Redd, what went on during those three nights Christ Jesus laid in the tomb?*"

The Earth Suit, Jesus, spent those three nights sleeping *(Luke 8:49-56)*. **Christ, The Spirit of life,** spent those three nights, *preaching unto* **THE SPIRITS IN PRISON***; Which **sometime** were disobedient, when once the longsuffering of God waited in the days of Noah, while the ark was a preparing, wherein few, that is, eight souls were saved by water (1Peter 3:19-20)*.

DEATH AND HELL

Christ went and preached to all those **SOMETIME** disobedient **THE SPIRITS IN PRISON** that refused to go into the Ark and be baptized with Noah and his household. Note, a **SOMETIME** disobedient believer is a lukewarm person. This passage reveals to us that Christ preached to the *spirits* of those people who lived in Noah's day; *spirits* in the prison cell of **Hell** that were disobedient and He is doing it again today through His body, the Church. Christ went before these disobedient *spirits* and proclaimed His triumph over **Death**. Confirming to them that the message preached by Noah should have been believed and proving to them that the faith which Noah possessed was a faith that transcends the world of **Death** and to us who believe in him, the world of **Hell**. Why? Because Noah's life and the proclamation of his faith in Himself went before the spirits of the men in those days and personally proclaimed the victory and one day He is going to return to our planet, the earth, and rapture His church out of this world as a sign to the unbelievers of this day's generation who continue to live in unbelief to the Word of God. Whose words were those that Noah was preaching to those spirits. It was God's. Whose words do preachers preach in the world today, God's.

Born again believers have got to remember that *John 1:13* tells us that our rebirth was *not of blood, nor of the will of the Flesh, nor of the will of man, but of God.* A rebirth mentioned in *1 Peter 1:23* that is carried out by the Word of God, which liveth and abideth for ever. Therefore, every born again believer that has put on Christ has got to *be sober, be vigilant; because your adversary the devil, as a roaring lion, walketh about, seeking whom he may devour (1 Peter 5:8).* Who are the ones he is seeking to devour? Those *whom resist stedfast in the faith (1 Peter 5:9).* That's why you and I need to *remain faithful unto Death (Rev 2:10)* and not allow the devil, the god of this world, to blind us to the truth that our water baptism in Jesus name buried us into **Death** and that we cannot die anymore. Why? Because our rebirth was from incorruptible seed. Incorruptible means, *"incapable of corruption: not subject to decay or dissolution: incapable of being bribed or morally corrupted."* The first Adam was corruptible, and he could die

104

(Gen 2:17). Christ was not. Therefore, after a person is baptized and receives Christ Jesus as Lord and Savior of their life, Christ gives that individual the power and right to become something he/she was formally not, **a child of God**. This new birth as mentioned in *2Cor 5:17* has nothing to do with human blood, the will of the **Flesh**, or by the will of highly esteemed men, to include those of us who are pastors. This new birth we receive of and by the Word of God is incorruptible and cannot die. So, let's look at *John 5:24* again, it reads,

*"Verily, verily, I say unto you, He that <u>heareth my word</u>, and believeth on him that sent me, hath everlasting life, and shall not come into condemnation; but is **passed from death unto <u>life</u>**."*

Notice, Jesus did not say doeth his word. It was His brother James in *James 1:22* who tells us to be doers. James says, *"be ye doers of the word, and not hearers only, deceiving your own selves"*. Jesus said, *<u>heareth his word</u>*. Believers are commanded to be hearers of the word for this is how we receive our faith as told to us in *Romans 10:17.* This verse says,

"So then faith cometh by hearing, and hearing by the word of God."

Furthermore, *Hebrews 11:6* says,

"But without faith it is impossible to please him: for he that cometh to God must believe that he is, and that he is a rewarder of them that diligently seek him."

Once a man or woman is born again, and receives God's engrafted word, which is able to save your souls *(<u>The word must save our souls, not ourselves Matt 10:39</u>)*, he/she must begin to walk in the newness of everlasting life, the Christ life *(Phil 1:21)*. It is **through this life** that believers receive their empowerment to obey the instructions ministered to us in *James 1:21*. A life that has been anointed with God's Holy Spirit that now has the preeminence over us as we *press toward the mark* *for the prize of the high calling of God in Christ Jesus (Philip. 3:14)* A life that *Acts 2:24* tells us **Death** cannot take hold of. Why? Because when *we were baptized into Jesus Christ we were baptized into his **Death**. Therefore we are buried with him by baptism into **Death**: that like as Christ was raised up from the dead by the glory of the Father, even so we also should walk in newness of life. For if we have been planted together in the likeness of his death, we shall be also in the likeness of his resurrection (Romans 6:3-5).*

Water Baptism *plants us together with Christ in the likeness of his **Death***. Therefore, we should be walking in the newness of spiritual life. A life of faith and obedience, built on a principle called **Love**; because it's going to take some strong faith to live a life of **Love** in this wicked world governed by the law of **Sin** *(Rom 7:14)*. Let's read *Romans 13:8* and *1John 3:14*. They read,

*"Owe no man any thing, but to love one another: for he that loveth another hath **fulfilled the law**."* And *"We know that **we have passed from death unto life, because we love the brethren**. **He that loveth not his brother abideth in Death**"*

Failure to believe in Jesus is the greatest mistake a person can make in life. The second greatest mistake is the mistake of thinking that we do not owe our fellow man anything. But, according to *Romans 13:8*, men and women owe *one another* love. Are you a man? Are you a woman? Then you are indebted to every man or woman you encounter. The perfect will of God refers to it as an unpayable debt and everyone is commanded to live according to this principle. For whosoever it be that *hears* this verse and obeys it, fulfils the requirements of the law. Remember, Jesus did not come to destroy the law; He came to fulfil *(Matthew 5:17)* it.

Now, *1John 3:14* is the verse I really want to expound on. It is the second verse in the Bible that gives us insight on how a person is passed from **Death** unto life. It reads, *"We know* *that we have passed from **Death** unto life, because we love the brethren. He that loveth not his brother abideth in **Death**".*

This verse along with the other verse, *John 5:24* should be fervently taught and discussed in weekly Bible Study settings until new converts as well as seasoned believers fully understand the importance of what the Apostle John desires for all men to *hear* and obey. Because judging by the messages we hear being preached and taught in church services today, anyone can see that only a few of our Pastors spend any *Time* meditating on these two verses to where they are able to truly teach the real meaning of them to those entrusted to their *Care (Luke 12:48).* Why? Because many of them have decided to spend their *Time* writing songs, doing concerts, or ministering on verses that address Old Testament ordinances or their ministry needs rather than addressing the problem of love that is lacking in the life of men and women who profess to be born again believers. There are just too many professing born again believers void of the agape love that *Matt 5:16* instructs believers to shine before the inhabitants of the earth and this Love-less life is going to cause many of them to spend *Time* in ***Hell*** if someone does not teach them the truths of the gospel *(Matt 28:20).*

Let's read a story told by Christ in Luke, Chapter 16. It is a true life story about a man who was a Son of Abraham that lived a love-less life towards his fellowman. Please note, this is not a parable, but a true life event and it reads on this wise,

"There was a certain rich man, which was clothed in purple and fine linen, and fared sumptuously every day: And there was a certain beggar named Lazarus, which was laid at his gate, full of sores, And desiring to be fed with the crumbs which fell from the rich man's table: moreover the dogs came and licked his sores. And it came to pass, that the beggar died, and was carried by the angels into Abraham's bosom: the rich man also died, and was buried; And in hell he lift up his eyes, being in torments, and seeth Abraham afar off, and Lazarus in his bosom. And he cried and said, Father Abraham, have mercy on me, and send Lazarus, that he may dip the tip of his finger in

water, and cool my tongue; for I am tormented in this flame. But Abraham said, Son, remember that thou in thy lifetime receivedst thy good things, and likewise Lazarus evil things: but now he is comforted, and thou art tormented. And beside all this, between us and you there is a great gulf fixed: so that they which would pass from hence to you cannot; neither can they pass to us, that would come from thence. Then he said, I pray thee therefore, father, that thou wouldest send him to my father's house: For I have five brethren; that he may testify unto them, lest they also come into this place of torment. Abraham saith unto him, They have Moses and the prophets; let them hear them. And he said, Nay, father Abraham: but if one went unto them from the dead, they will repent. And he said unto him, If they hear not Moses and the prophets, neither will they be persuaded, though one rose from the dead."

The rich man and Lazarus were descendants of Abraham. All Israelites come from the bosom of Abraham *(Hebrews 7:5)*, who is alive according to this story and according to *Mark 12:26-27*, he is alive. Yes, Abraham's earth suit has dead and awaiting resurrection *(1Thes 4:16)* but the Word of God says he is alive. IN this story, Jesus takes us on the other side of **Death** and gives us insight on Abraham's bosom and what it represented prior to Christ dying for the **Sin's** of men. Abraham's bosom became a holding cell for all his children who died awaiting the promise of the Lord's Christ *(Luke 2:25-29)*. On the other hand, Abraham's descendants who refused to love their fellow man, especially those of the same household *(Gal 6:10)*, went to **Hell**, Not **Death**. Why? Because Abraham is alive and those born of his womb are the offspring of a man who was born of incorruptible seed. Abram *(Gen 12:1)*, the person born in the image of the first man Adam to Terah *(Gen 11:27)*, was corruptible. So, because these two men were descendants of Abraham and not Abram, they passed completely through the holding cell of **Death** when they died and into ***Life*** and ***Hell***. Have you never read *Matthew 10:28?* It reads,

*"And fear not them which kill the body, but are not able to kill the soul: but rather fear him which is able to destroy both soul and body in **Hell**."*

Most believers who do not understand this verse. What makes me say this? Believers fear **Death**. I pray that what I am about to write will comfort you in this area of your life. **Death** is that *which kill the body*. It cannot kill the soul. Why? First, the soul is not made of a mineral from this world, only our earthen vessel *(Gen 2:7)*. Secondly, let's read *Romans 6:4* again. It reads, *"Therefore we are buried with him by baptism into* ***Death***.*"* Water baptism buries men into **Death**. The believer has no need to fear **Death** but he/she better fear **Hell** and the one *which is able to destroy both soul and body in it*. Something that this rich man and thousands of born again believers who harden their necks after being often reproved *(Prov 29:1)* shall abide if they die before Christ raptures the Church **(true worshippers John 4:23)** out of this world *(John 4:23)*.

Please notice, this rich man was not a Gentile, he called Abraham, Father. Abraham is not the father of Gentiles. Abram was *(Gen 16:15)*, but not Abraham. God changed Abram's name to Abraham in *Genesis 17: 5-14* when He covenanted with Abraham. The Gentiles are a nation of people God never covenanted with. They are people who are alienated from the life of God *(Eph 4:18)*. The Israelites, Abraham's seed are not so *(Eph 2:11-12)*. Therefore, the rich man, should have **Cared** for Lazarus and not let the opportunity for him to love or do good *(James 4:17)* unto Lazarus pass him by. Let's read *1John 3:17*. It reads,

"But whoso hath this world's good, and seeth his brother have need, and shutteth up his bowels of compassion from him, how dwelleth the love of God in him?"

The rich man possessed *this world's goods and fared sumptuously everyday* **(extravagantly, he lived a good life)**. I know a lot of believers whose lives mirror the life of this rich man, does yours? I know this rich man was aware that Lazarus *laid at his gate desiring to be fed with the crumbs which fell from the rich man's table.* How do I know this? He said Lazarus' name to Abraham. This proves that not only did he know he was there but knew who he was *(Father Abraham, have mercy on me, and send Lazarus, that he may dip the tip of his finger in water, and cool my tongue).* Furthermore, Lazarus is identified as a beggar. Now, during some of my military deployments outside of the United States, I encountered some diligent beggars. Beggars that will not leave you alone and will make sure you know they are there. This rich man knew Lazarus was there yet refused to give Lazarus *the crumbs which fell from his table (Even Jesus fed the beggar woman who desired of Him to save her daughter and He provided her with more than crumbs Matt 15:22-28).* This rich man gave Lazarus nothing. Nevertheless, I will commend this rich man in one area of his life. At least he didn't call the police on Lazarus. In the world we live in today, most people, believers too, would not allow this. Oh no. We *Care* too much about ourselves, homes, cars, and our other possessions to let someone such as Lazarus impose upon our sumptuous, prosperous lifestyles. Furthermore, the rich man's refusal to acknowledge and show *Love* towards Lazarus isn't even considered a *Sin* in the eyes of the world today. Civilization today recognizes this as a trespass on Lazarus' part instead of realizing that according to *Romans 13:8*, we are the ones in the trespass. You do remember that verse don't you? I'll write it again. It reads, *"Owe no man any thing, but to love one another: for he that loveth another hath fulfilled the law."* Those who fail to live according to the principle of this verse are trespassing against the law of *Love*. A believer's love reveals to God whether or not that believer has been born again of God's incorruptible seed. The seed that enables a believer to pass from *Death* unto life and the proof that that believer *is born of God*. Let's read *1John 4:7-8 and 21*, they read,

"Beloved, let us love one another: for love is of God; and every one that loveth is born of God, and knoweth God. He that loveth not knoweth not God; for God is love" And *"And this commandment have we from him, That he who loveth God love his brother also."*

Love is of God; everyone that loveth is born of God and knoweth God. The rich man did not show Lazarus any love. Do you behave in this manner? If you do, then look at what happens. When both men's appointment with **Death** arrived *(Hebrews 9:27)*, and despite the *fact* that both were descendants of Abraham, each went to a different holding cells. The Angels carried Lazarus into Abraham's Bosom *(life)*. Nowhere in those verses does it say that Lazarus was buried. Why? Jesus will never associated a person of life with burial. We do not hold burials for the living; we hold them for the dead. However, the rich man was buried, and went into **_Hell_**, not **Death**. Why not **Death**? He came out of Abraham's bosom. Is Abraham Dead? No. He was an Israelite. Look at what *Romans 9:4* says about Israelites. It says,

"Who are Israelites; to whom pertaineth the adoption, and the glory, and the covenants, and the giving of the law, and the service of God, and the promises".

Israelites were a greatly privileged people, a people who had been highly favored by God because of their father Abraham. In this story, Jesus truly blesses us by showing us the eternal justice given to those who are the children of those in a covenant relationship with God and their life after **Death**. We who have been baptized share in this same type of relationship just as these two men because we all have been born again of incorruptible seed and have one Father (*John 20:17)*.

Let's continue, Lazarus is known. He has a name. The rich man is also known but does not have a name. Why does this rich man not have a name? He does not have a name because he did not **Love**. Remember *He that loveth not knoweth not God*. Because the rich man did not know love means that he did not know God. Since he did not know God means that he could not love God and according to *1Cor 8:3*, *"But if any man love God, the same is known of him"*, since he did not love God, then he was nameless to God thereby eliminating any chance of God being able to save him. Lazarus knew God and was known of God. Lazarus must have been a man of **Love** and because he

Loved, God knew him. However, the god of this world, Satan, made sure that Lazarus received nothing good in his lifetime during his days on the earth simply because he loved. God probably put Lazarus *(Heb 13:2)* at the rich man's gate to show the rich man the wickedness of his heart *(Jer 17:9)* in hopes that he would repent and be saved *(1John 1:9)* but the rich man ignored every opportunity he was given to be a blessing to Lazarus. The thought of giving Lazarus **_something_** never crossed his mind. Nor did the though cross his mind that God just might be using Lazarus as a vessel to show him the errors of his ways *(James 5:20)*. Are you like this rich man? Are you nameless to God? Do you *fare sumptuously every day?* Professing Christians, do you have this world's goods? How often have you felt suffering? This question is addressed to all Christians, even the ones who have a small amount of money, including myself. Who do you see suffering? What's stopping you from helping the one's who are in need? Hear what the Lord says in *Matthew 25:31-40*. He says,

"*When the Son of man shall come in his glory, and all the holy angels with him, then shall he sit upon the throne of his glory: And before him shall be gathered all nations: and he shall separate them one from another, as a shepherd divideth his sheep from the goats: And he shall set the sheep on his right hand, but the goats on the left. Then shall the King say unto them on his right hand, Come, ye blessed of my Father, inherit the kingdom prepared for you from the foundation of the world: For I was an hungred, and ye gave me meat: I was thirsty, and ye gave me drink: I was a stranger, and ye took me in: Naked, and ye clothed me: I was sick, and ye visited me: I was in prison, and ye came unto me. Then shall the righteous answer him, saying, Lord, when saw we thee an hungred, and fed thee? or thirsty, and gave thee drink? When saw we thee a stranger, and took thee in? or naked, and clothed thee? Or when saw we thee sick, or in prison, and came unto thee? And the King shall answer and say unto them, Verily I say unto you, **Inasmuch as ye have done it unto one of the least of these my brethren**, ye have done it unto me*".

You are not the only person suffering. Everyone living in this world suffers at sometime. But, in this story, no where is it mentioned that this rich man or his brethren suffer. My prayer is that you will see where this rich man went and his brothers are heading to that same holding cell if they do not humble themselves, and pray, and seek the LORD's face, and turn from their wicked ways; so that the LORD may hear from heaven, and forgive their **Sins**, and heal their land *(2 Chron. 7:14)*. Furthermore, look at what Jesus told his disciples, not unbelievers in *Matthew 16: 15-18*,

> *"He saith unto them, But whom say ye that I am? And Simon Peter answered and said, Thou art the Christ, the Son of the living God. And Jesus answered and said unto him, Blessed art thou, Simon Barjona: for flesh and blood hath not revealed it unto thee, but my Father which is in heaven. And I say also unto thee, That thou art Peter, and upon this rock I will build my church; and the gates of hell shall not prevail against it."*

Christ overcame **Death**. We who are in Christ have also overcome **Death** but we have not overcome **Hell**. Only our obedience to the scriptures *(2Tim 3:16)* and our love for men enables us to overcome Satan and the gates of **Hell**. The rich man did neither of these, what about you? Christians, Judgment Day will begin at the church first. In *1Timothy 3:15*, Paul says,

> *"But if I tarry long, that thou mayest know how thou oughtest to behave thyself in the house of God, which is the church of the living God, the pillar and ground of the truth."*

And Peter says in *1 Peter 4:17*,

> *"For the time is come that **judgment** must begin at the house of God: and if it first begin at us, what shall the end be of them that obey not the gospel of God?"*

We as saints know how we ought to be living since Christ has become our life. If you do not know *how thou oughtest to behave thyself* as sons of God *(Romans 8:14)* and you die before the rapture, in **_Hell_** you will lift up your eyes _(Luke 16:23)._

What is **_Hell_**? It is not the lake of fire as men portray it to be; it is a holding cell. A place of torments _(Luke 16:23)_ the Lord warns us about in this story and the place trying to prevail against the Church, not you. However, it is we who make up the church. Remember, Jesus told Peter that the gates of **_Hell_** would not prevail against the church. Therefore, if you do not overcome these gates when they come to test you, then there is only one place you can go and that is through the gates of **_Hell_** because the gates of **_Hell_** is the thing trying to overcome you. You cannot go into **_Death_**. Let's read _1 Peter 4: 12-14_, they read,

"Beloved, think it not strange concerning the fiery trial which is to try you, as though some strange thing happened unto you: But rejoice, inasmuch as ye are partakers of Christ's sufferings; that, when his glory shall be revealed, ye may be glad also with exceeding joy. If ye be reproached for the name of Christ, happy are ye; for the spirit of glory and of God resteth upon you: on their part he is evil spoken of, but on your part he is glorified."

The tests are coming. The devil isn't letting you go that easy. He's going to try and get you to worship him _(Matthew 4: 8-11)_. Satan is going to throw everything at you. He starts by making you look at the outer appearance of other men until you stop loving or forgiving them and when you stop loving or forgiving men, you as a believer have been overcome and have become once again, a servant of **_Sin_**. I did not say that you became a sinner again, you were born of incorruptible seed, but I will say that you are serving **_Sin_** _(Matt 6:14-15)_. After you are born of the Spirit, you are Spirit _(John 3:6)_ and you answer to the Lord and _oughtest to behave thyself_ obediently now that you are a child of God _(Rom 8:16)_ and a servant of God and of the Lord Jesus Christ _(James 1:1)_. Look at what Jesus says in _John 15:20_, when he said,

"*Remember the word that I said unto you, The servant is not greater than his lord. If they have persecuted me, they will also persecute you; if they have kept my saying, they will keep yours also.*"

Does persecution quench the zeal you have for God to a state of lukewarmness? Does persecution cause you to stop loving your fellow man? I pray that it does not. Look at what *the Amen, the faithful and true witness, the beginning of the creation of God* spake unto the church of the Laodiceans in *Revelation 3: 14-16*,

"*And unto the angel of the church of the Laodiceans write; These things saith the Amen, the faithful and true witness, the beginning of the creation of God; I know thy works, that thou art neither cold nor hot: I would thou wert cold or hot. So then **because thou art lukewarm**, and neither cold nor hot, I will spue thee out of my mouth.*"

We as believers must not allow persecution to make us **lukewarm** or "a **SOMETIME** obedient/disobedient individual". Lukewarmness means that you are warm enough for true worshippers *(John 4:23)* to think that you stand for Christ but cold enough for the unbeliever to think that he or she can do or say anything in your atmosphere with the confidence that you will not separate yourself from them no matter how they *behave* themselves. Therefore, **because thou art lukewarm**, Christ is going to *spue thee out of his mouth*.

Some of **us** *(me too)* go to church all the time and talk the talk all the time in the presence of the saints but when persecution arises, we change. This in turn causes us to become ashamed *(Romans 1:16-17)* and afraid *(Prov 6:2)* to stand up for Christ and we become lukewarm. This is lukewarmness and this lukewarmness positions us as believers to be spued out of Christ's mouth. Let me say something. I am often reproved of God on this matter. One day I heard His voice asking me a question. The question was, "**Minister Redd, you need to make up your mind as to what you are going to be Son. Is it hot or** *cold, because you do them both so well?*" I do not ever want to hear that again. It wasn't the voice of Satan I can assure you of that because I am sure Satan did not want me to know that.

Where do you think the LORD God will spue us out to? Not **Death**! **Death** cannot hold us; we have been born again of the spirit, of incorruptible seed. Therefore, we Christians must stop being ashamed to let unbelievers know that we are new creatures in Christ Jesus *(2Cor 5:17)* and be willing to suffer whatever backlash the unbelievers of this world dish out to us. Furthermore, every time you find yourself in a trial that causes you to suffer as a Christian *(1Peter 4:16)* and you become ashamed of Christ, then Mark 8:38 has some words for you. It says,

"*Whosoever therefore shall be ashamed of me and of my words in this adulterous and sinful generation; of him also shall the Son of man be ashamed, when he cometh in the glory of his Father with the holy angels.*"

When you are persecuted, please do not become ashamed of Christ for if you do, then the chances of Him spewing you out of His mouth are increased. But like I said before, even if He does spue us out of His mouth, it will not be in to **Death**. The entire 28th chapter of Matthew is addressed to Christ's disciples. Yet, Jesus does not mention **Death** to them or what **Death** could do to them in any of those verses. Life never talks about **Death**, especially when Christ told them *He came that they might have life, and have it more abundantly (John 10:10)*. When Jesus started His ministry, He started by saying, *I must preach the kingdom of God; for therefore am I sent (Luke 4:43).* However, He used some of His **Time** to speak about a place that we as believers need to be aware of, a place called **Hell**.

Hell is the word that our LORD and Saviour refers to when addressing the church. In St. Mark, Chapter 9, Jesus addresses His disciple again and in verse 35-50 says,

"*And he sat down, and called the twelve, and saith unto them, If any man desire to be first, the same shall be last of all, and servant of all. And he took a child, and set him in the midst of them: and when he had taken him in his arms, he said unto them, Whosoever shall receive one of such children in my name, receiveth me: and whosoever shall receive me, receiveth not me, but him that sent me. And John answered him, saying, Master, we saw one casting out devils in thy name, and he followeth not us: and we forbad him, because he followeth not us. But Jesus said, Forbid him not: for there is no man which shall do a miracle in my name, that can lightly speak evil of me. For he that is not against us is on our part. For whosoever shall give you a cup of water to drink in my name, because ye belong to Christ, verily I say unto you, he shall not lose his reward* (Rich Man and Lazarus) *And whosoever shall offend one of these little ones that believe in me*, it is better for him that a millstone were hanged about his neck, and he were cast into the sea. And if thy hand offend thee, cut it off: it is better for thee to enter into life maimed, than having two hands to go into **hell**, into the fire that never shall be quenched: Where their worm dieth not, and the fire is not quenched. And if thy foot offend thee, cut it off: it is better for thee to enter halt into life, than having two feet to be cast into **hell**, into the fire that never shall be quenched: Where their worm dieth not, and the fire is not quenched. And if thine eye offend thee, pluck it out: it is better for thee to enter into the kingdom of God with one eye, than having two eyes to be cast into **hell** fire: Where their worm dieth not, and the fire is not quenched. For every one shall be salted with fire, and every sacrifice shall be salted with salt. Salt is good: but if the salt have lost his saltness, wherewith will ye season it? Have salt in yourselves, and have peace one with another.*"

Jesus calls his disciples and tells them about offending baby believers. To offend means to "*hurt the feelings of, to insult*". I do not know why I am writing this in this book, I know you do not do this, do you? Well, if you do, then please look at what the Lord recommends you do with the body part that is doing the offending. *Furthermore, please know that Christ is speaking spiritual here, not carnal. Don't go cutting of body parts*. Christ is making reference to something in a believers life that will cause their whole body to be *cast into **Hell***? It doesn't matter to me whether you believe me or not, which is something the Devil hopes you will do anyway. Nevertheless, I am clearly portraying for you what our LORD wants and needs every Christian to understand in regards to ***Hell*** and its relevance to born again believers. Christ needs for us to understand that ***Hell*** is the holding cell for disobedient born again believers who die before the Lord's return in *1Thes 4:13-18*.

Let's talk about ***Hell***. What is ***Hell*** fire? What are the worms that die not? What is that salt?

Hell fire is exactly what Sister Stacie is talking about in her paragraph at the front of this book. It is the absence of God's presence to the one who once enjoy the presence and glory of it. Let's read *Jonah, Chapter 1:1-17, 2:1-2*. It reads,

*"Now the word of the LORD came unto Jonah the son of Amittai, saying, Arise, go to Nineveh, that great city, and cry against it; for their wickedness is come up before me. **But Jonah rose up to flee unto Tarshish from the presence of the LORD**, and went down to Joppa; and he found a ship going to Tarshish: so he paid the fare thereof, and went down into it, to go with them unto Tarshish from the presence of the LORD. But the LORD sent out a great wind into the sea, and there was a mighty tempest in the sea, so that the ship was like to be broken. Then the mariners were afraid, and cried every man unto his god, and cast forth the wares that were in the ship into the sea, to lighten it of them. But Jonah was gone down into the sides of the ship; and he lay, and was fast asleep. So the shipmaster came to him, and said unto him, What meanest thou, O sleeper? Arise, call upon thy God, if so be that God will think upon us, that we perish not. And they said every one to his fellow, Come, and let us cast lots, that we may know for whose cause this evil is upon us. So they cast lots, and the lot fell upon Jonah. Then said they unto him, Tell us, we pray thee, for whose cause this evil is upon us; What is thine occupation? and whence comest thou? what is thy country? and of what people art thou? And he said unto them, I*

am an Hebrew; and I fear the LORD, the God of heaven, which hath made the sea and the dry land. Then were the men exceedingly afraid, and said unto him, Why hast thou done this? **_For the men knew that he fled from the presence of the LORD_***, because he had told them. Then said they unto him, What shall we do unto thee, that the sea may be calm unto us? for the sea wrought, and was tempestuous. And he said unto them, Take me up, and cast me forth into the sea; so shall the sea be calm unto you: for I know that for my sake this great tempest is upon you. Nevertheless the men rowed hard to bring it to the land; but they could not: for the sea wrought, and was tempestuous against them. Wherefore they cried unto the LORD, and said, We beseech thee, O LORD, we beseech thee, let us not perish for this man's life, and lay not upon us innocent blood: for thou, O LORD, hast done as it pleased thee. So they took up Jonah, and cast him forth into the sea: and the sea ceased from her raging. Then the men feared the LORD exceedingly, and offered a sacrifice unto the LORD, and made vows.* _Now the LORD had prepared a great fish to swallow up Jonah. And Jonah was in the belly of the fish three days and three nights. Then Jonah prayed unto the LORD his God out of the fish's belly, And said, I cried by reason of mine affliction unto the LORD, and he heard me;_ **_out of the belly of Hell cried I, and thou heardest my voice._**"

You do not get to decide where you will spend your life when you flee from the presence of the LORD or when you die. Ask the first man Adam and Eve *(Genesis 3:23-24)*. Ask the Angels which kept not their first estate *(Jude 6)*. No, ask the rich man that brought forth plentifully in *Luke 12:16-21*. The Lord God decides where you will spend your life and He prepares a place for you. ***There is nothing secretive about this***. Throughout the Bible, the Lord God has always prepared a place for those who disobey *His teachings and sayings*, including disobedient children of the kingdom. We always hear about the fate of unbelievers, but in *Matthew 8:12*, the Lord addresses the children of the kingdom. It reads,

*But **the children of the kingdom** shall be cast out into outer darkness: there shall be weeping and gnashing of teeth.*

Do you see that? ***The children of the kingdom*** *shall be cast out into outer darkness.* This means that these children must have previously been children of Light. Not every Israelite that left out of Egypt was obedient. In addition, *Eph 5:8* says, *"For ye were sometimes darkness, but now are ye light in the Lord: walk as children of light."* Have you stopped walking as *children of light* and become dark again. If you have then you better heed that verse. There came a day in the life of Jonah when he let Sin darken his mind to the Will of God.

From this story about Jonah, let's focus our attention on three days of Jonah's life and look at the holding cell the Lord prepared for Jonah when Jonah fled from His presence? In the day when Jonah left from a *commandment of the Lord.* A day when Jonah became lukewarm towards the Word of God.

Now the LORD had prepared a great fish to swallow up Jonah. Do you ever feel like you've been swallowed up by something? I do. What did Jonah call this great fish that swallowed him which made him cry out of the belly of it? ***Hell.*** Not ***Death*** but ***Hell.*** Jonah's failure to submit himself to *the sayings of the Lord* caused the Lord to put him in a holding cell; a holding cell that kept him away from the ***presence of the LORD*** and he cried unto the Lord to be delivered from it. Thank goodness the LORD had mercy on him. The Lord is manifesting this same type of mercy on a lot us believers today as we daily rebel against His *sayings and teachings* that tells us *the Father seeketh true worshippers that will worship him in spirit and in truth* (John 4:23). People who love and forgive their fellowman.

When Jonah failed to live this, the Lord prepared a big fish for him and it swallowed him up. While Jonah was in the belly of this fish, he sorely missed the Lord's presence and nobody can describe the Lord's presence, something that I think nobody can describe better than Jeremiah. Jeremiah says in *Jeremiah 20:9* that, *"His word was in mine heart as a burning fire shut up in my bones".* I can assure you that this same word was in Jonah, why didn't he obey it. Why won't we obey it? We like Jonah refuse to obey it when we fail to reckon our body of

Sin as dead. Anyone who leaves the presence of the Lord will burn for the Lord's presence once more. This is what the rich man wanted. Once he became separated from the sumptuous lifestyle he lived while on the earth, he was burning to taste it again. That was the torment he was in. **_Hell_** torments the soul; it is not a physical fire. If the rich man had been in a physical fire, he would have asked Abraham to make Lazarus give him more than just water for his tongue. During his life on the earth, he never knew what it was like to be hungry, to be thirsty, to be cold, lonely, and unwanted. **_For him_**, to experience a life of this magnitude gives the greatest picture of what **_Hell_** is and judging by the way most believers are _behaving_ today, this is what the future holds for them. The rich man knew his brothers were on their way to **_Hell_** and so are many of us. What makes me say this? _Matthew 8:12_. It reads,

"*But the children of the kingdom shall be cast out into outer darkness: there shall be weeping and gnashing of teeth.*"

Let's look at *Acts 12, verse 1 and 21-23*. Verses that address the life of Jewish king, a son of King David. It says,

"*Now about that time Herod the king stretched forth his hands to vex certain of the church.*" And "*And upon a set day Herod, arrayed in royal apparel, sat upon his throne, and made an oration unto them. And the people gave a shout, saying, It is the voice of a god, and not of a man. And immediately the angel of the Lord smote him, because he gave not God the glory: and he was eaten of worms, and gave up the ghost.*"

Herod was a Jewish king, an Israelite. A man born from the only nation God ever covenanted with. A man from the loins of King David. This King was vexing the church of God and because he did not give glory unto God as his father King David did but chose to take God's glory upon himself. Well, Upon him doing this, an Angel of the Lord smote him and he was eaten of worms. Child of God, if we do not give God the glory due His name, per chance, an _angel of the Lord might smote_ us. If he smites us with the same frame of mind that Herod had, we will go to ***Hell*** and rot where the worm dieth not and the presence of the Lord delivers us not. Herod and the rich man are living examples of what happens when a believer neglects to obey the <u>*saying and teachings*</u> of Christ or love the brethren *(1John 3: 14)*. Let's read <u>*Hebrews 2:3*</u>. It says,

"*<u>How shall we escape, if we neglect so great salvation</u>; which at the first began to be spoken by the Lord, and was confirmed unto us by them that heard him.*"

Believers love to ask the question, "*If you are once saved, are you always saved?*" <u>*Hebrews 2:3*</u> answers that for us. God saved Lot and his family but did Mrs. Lot remain saved? Once saved, always saved, <u>*yes*</u>. Neglecting your salvation Is another thing. Mrs. Lot neglected her salvation. King Herod neglected his salvation. Neglect means, "<u>*to pay no attention or too little attention to; disregard or slight: to fail to carry out or perform (orders, duties, etc.): to be remiss in the care or treatment of*</u>."

Let me put this verse and <u>*Matthew 10:28*</u> together. They read,

"*<u>How shall we escape</u>*, if we neglect so great salvation; which at the first began to be spoken by the Lord, and was confirmed unto us by them that heard him" and "fear not them which kill the body, but are not able to kill the soul: but rather fear him which is able to destroy both soul and body in ***Hell***."

Believers do not have to worry about escaping Death, we have been passed from Death. However, you have not escaped Hell. You can neglect what our Lord said about ***Hell***, about worshipping God in spirit and in truth, and about loving your fellow man, but you will not escape Hell if you become lukewarm and fail to obey his voice *(John 10:27-29)*. Please read <u>*John 10:27-29*</u> before you read further. Did you know that after you were baptized in Jesus name and accepted Christ as your life that you became His sheep? Well, since you know this, how does your life in Christ measure when line up against the scriptures *(Isaiah 28:10-13)*.

The LORD loves the human race and *is not slack concerning his promise, even though some men count slackness; but is longsuffering to us-ward, not willing that any should perish, but that all should come to repentance (2 Peter 3:9)*. The Lord wants us to come to repentance, and He is longsuffering towards us, waiting for us to worship the Father in Spirit and in truth. Waiting for us to apply the principle of love to our lives. He has no desire to see you make *Hell* your home; you make that choice. The first man Adam and Eve made theirs, the rich man made his, Mrs. Lot made hers. *Death* can't hold you. Water baptism passed you through *Death*, this leaves only one place for you and I as believers to go, *Hell*. So, please do not harden your neck when *the sayings and teachings* of the Lord reprove you when you err in the way *(James 5:19-20)*, because if you do, you will be destroyed as King Herod, Mrs. Lot, and other salvation neglectors of the Bible did. Let's read *Proverbs 29:1*, it reads,

"He, that being often reproved hardeneth his neck, shall suddenly be destroyed, and that without remedy."

If you constantly *(often)* rebel *(hardeneth)* against the *sayings and teachings of the Lord*, you will be destroyed. Where? In *Hell*. *"Fear him which is able to destroy both soul and body in Hell (Matt 10:28)"*. That my Christian brothers and sisters according to this verse will be without remedy. And at the end of *Time,* when the Lord returns to judge the world, *whosoever's name not found written in the book of life shall be cast into the lake of fire (Rev. 20:15)*. Let's look at Revelation 20:11-15. These verses read,

*And I saw a great white throne, and him that sat on it, from whose **face the earth and the heaven fled away**; and there was found no place for them. [12] And I saw the dead, small and great, stand before God; and the books were opened: and another book was opened, which is the book of life: and the dead were judged out of those things which were written in the books,* *according to their works. [13] And the sea gave up the dead which were in it; and* **death and hell delivered up the dead which were in them**: *and they were judged every man according to their works. [14] And* **death and hell were cast into the lake of fire.** *This is the second death. [15] And whosoever was not found written in the book of life was cast into the lake of fire.*

I will end this book with questions. Questions that your Pastor should be able to give you clarity on. If not, my email address is Redd@christ-our-life.org, I would be honored to answer any question you may have.

1. *What happens to Heaven and the Earth in these verses?* Well, you can't live there.

2. *The holding cells, what was in Death? What was in **Hell**?*

3. *Where was Death and Hell Cast?* If so, then why do people say that **Hell** is the lake of fire if it is being cast into the lake of fire?

I pray that you have been blessed by this book and that God uses this book to prepare for himself a people who are true worshippers.

Printed in the United States
214358BV00001B/6/P

9 781600 471711